Philosophy of Logic

PHILOSOPHY
OF LOGIC
Second Edition

W. V. Quine

Harvard University Press
Cambridge, Massachusetts
and London, England
1986

Copyright © 1970, 1986 by W. V. Quine
All rights reserved
Printed in the United States of America
10 9 8 7 6 5 4 3 2 1

Library of Congress Cataloging-in-Publication Data

Quine, W. V. (Willard Van Orman)
    Philosophy of logic.

    Bibliography: p.
    Includes index.
    1. Logic.   2. Philosophy.   I. Title
 BC51.Q5   1986   160   85-24734
ISBN 0-674-66563-5

To my daughter
Elizabeth Roberts

PREFACE, 1986

"Contrariwise," continued Tweedledee, "if it was so, it might be; and
if it were so, it would be; but as it isn't, it ain't. That's logic."
                                                            — Lewis Carroll

We shall be occupied in this book with the philosophy of logic
in substantially Tweedledee's sense of the word 'logic'. This is not
the invariable sense of the word. Precedent could be cited for applying the word collectively to two dissimilar studies: deductive and
inductive logic. The philosophy of inductive logic, however, would
be in no way distinguishable from philosophy's main stem, the theory of knowledge. What calls for a distinctive bit of philosophy is
deductive logic, the discipline that Tweedledee had in mind.

If pressed to supplement Tweedledee's ostensive definition of
logic with a discursive definition of the same subject, I would say
that logic is the systematic study of the logical truths. Pressed further,
I would say to read this book.

Since I see logic as the resultant of two components, truth and
grammar, I shall treat truth and grammar prominently. But I shall
argue against the doctrine that the logical truths are true because of
grammar, or because of language.

The notions of proposition and meaning will receive adverse
treatment. Set theory will be compared and contrasted with logic,
and ways will be examined of disguising each to resemble the other.
The status and claims of alternative logics will be discussed, and
reasons will be adduced for being thankful for what we have.

The book was sparked by two invitations in 1968: one from Professors Elizabeth and Monroe Beardsley to write a book on philosophy of logic for their Foundations of Philosophy series, and one from the Collège de France to give twelve lectures on *la philosophie de la logique*. I completed a draft of the book and then settled down to derive my French lectures. The book improved in the French version, so I subsequently revised the English version, working from the French.

Early drafts were helpfully criticized by George Boolos and Burton Dreben. Spot corrections of later printings were prompted by John Corcoran, Ruth Marcus, J. J. C. Smart, Masao Yamashita, and readers cited in the text.

Further reflection has now led me again to insert or rewrite various scattered paragraphs, sufficient perhaps to warrant the title of second edition. Altogether the main changes made in this edition and in the course of earlier printings are in pages 4–5, 36–38, 50, 59–60, 68, 93–94, and 100.

W. V. QUINE

CONTENTS

Philosophy of Logic

MEANING AND TRUTH

1

When someone speaks truly, what makes his statement true?
We tend to feel that there are two factors: meaning and fact.

A German utters a declarative sentence: 'Der Schnee ist weiss.'
In so doing he speaks truly, thanks to the happy concurrence of
two circumstances: his sentence means that snow is white, and in
point of fact snow *is* white. If meanings had been different, if
'weiss' had meant green, then in uttering what he did he would not
have spoken truly. If the facts had been different, if snow had been
red, then again he would not have spoken truly.

What I have just said has a reassuring air of platitude about
it, and at the same time it shows disturbing signs of philosophical
extravagance. The German utters his declarative sentence; also there
is this white snow all around; so far so good. But must we go on and
appeal also to intangible intervening elements, a meaning and a
fact? The *meaning* of the *sentence* is that snow is white, and the
fact of the *matter* is that snow is white. The meaning of the sentence
and the fact of the matter here are apparently identical, or at any
rate they have the same name: that snow is white. And it is apparently because of this identity, or homonymy, that the German
may be said to have spoken truly. His meaning matches the fact.

This has the ring of a correspondence theory of truth, but as
a theory it is a hollow mockery. The correspondence holds only
between two intangibles that we have invoked as intervening elements between the German sentence and the white snow.

Someone may protest that I am being too severely literalistic about this seeming invocation of intervening elements. He may protest that when we speak of meaning as a factor in the truth of what the German said, we are merely saying, somewhat figuratively, what nobody can deny; namely, that if, for instance, the word 'weiss' were applied in German to green things instead of white ones, then what the German said about snow would have been false. He may protest likewise that the seeming reference to a fact, as something over and above the snow and its color, is only a manner of speaking.

Very well; as long as we can view matters thus, I have no complaint. But there has long been a strong trend in the philosophy of logic that cannot be thus excused. It is on meanings of sentences, rather than on facts, that this trend has offended most. Meanings of sentences are exalted as abstract entities in their own right, under the name of *propositions*. These, not the sentences themselves, are seen as the things that are true or false. These are the things also that stand in the logical relation of implication. These are the things also that are known or believed or disbelieved and are found obvious or surprising.

Philosophers' tolerance toward propositions has been encouraged partly by ambiguity in the term 'proposition'. The term often is used simply for the sentences themselves, declarative sentences; and then some writers who do use the term for meanings of sentences are careless about the distinction between sentences and their meanings. In inveighing against propositions in ensuing pages, I shall of course be inveighing against them always in the sense of sentence meanings.

Some philosophers, commendably diffident about positing propositions in this bold sense, have taken refuge in the word 'statement'. The opening question of this chapter illustrates this evasive use. My inveterate use of 'statement' in earlier books does not; I there used the word merely to refer to declarative sentences, and said so. Later I gave up the word in the face of the growing tendency at Oxford to use the word for acts that we perform in uttering declarative sentences. Now by appealing to statements in such a sense, instead of to propositions, certainly no clarity is gained. I shall say no more about statements, but will go on about propositions.

Once a philosopher, whether through inattention to ambiguity or simply through an excess of hospitality, has admitted propositions to his ontology, he invariably proceeds to view propositions rather than sentences as the things that are true and false. He feels he thereby gains directness, saving a step. Thus let us recall the German. He spoke truly, we saw, inasmuch as (1) 'Der Schnee ist weiss' means that the snow is white and (2) snow *is* white. Now our propositionalist saves step (1). The proposition, that snow is white, is true simply inasmuch as (2) snow *is* white. The propositionalist bypasses differences between languages; also differences of formulation within a language.

My objection to recognizing propositions does not arise primarily from philosophical parsimony—from a desire to dream of no more things in heaven and earth than need be. Nor does it arise, more specifically, from particularism—from a disapproval of intangible or abstract entities. My objection is more urgent. If there were propositions, they would induce a certain relation of synonymy or equivalence between sentences themselves: those sentences would be equivalent that expressed the same proposition. Now my objection is going to be that the appropriate equivalence relation makes no objective sense at the level of sentences. This, if I succeed in making it plain, should spike the hypothesis of propositions.

Propositions as Information
It is commonplace to speak of sentences as alike or unlike in meaning. This is such everyday, unphilosophical usage that it is apt to seem clearer than it really is. In fact it is vague, and the force of it varies excessively with the special needs of the moment. Thus suppose we are reporting a man's remark in indirect quotation. We are supposed to supply a sentence that is like his in meaning. In such a case we may be counted guilty of distorting his meaning when we so much as substitute a derogatory word for a neutral word having the same reference. Our substitution misrepresents his attitude and, therewith, his meaning. Yet on another occasion, where the interest is in relaying objective information without regard to attitudes, our substitution of the derogatory word for the neutral one will not be counted as distorting the man's meaning. Similar shifting of standards of likeness of meaning is evident in literary translation, according as our interest is in the poetic qualities of the passage or in the objective information conveyed.

The kind of likeness of meaning that is relevant to our present concerns, namely sameness of proposition, is the second of the alternatives mentioned in each of these examples. It is sameness of objective information, without regard to attitudes or to poetic qualities. If the notion of objective information were itself acceptably clear, there would be no quarrel with propositions.

The notion of information is indeed clear enough, nowadays, when properly relativized. It is central to the theory of communication. It makes sense relative to one or another preassigned matrix of alternatives—one or another checklist. You have to say in advance what features are going to count. Thus consider the familiar halftone method of photographic illustration. There is a screen, say six by six inches, containing a square array of regularly spaced positions, say a hundred to the inch in rows and columns.. A halftone picture is completely determined by settling which of these 360,000 points are black. Relative to this screen as the matrix of alternatives, information consists in saying which places are black. Two paintings give the same information, relative to this matrix, when they determine the same points as black. Differences in color are, so to speak, purely stylistic relative to this matrix; they convey no information. The case is similar even for differences in shape or position, when these are too slight to be registered in the dots of the halftone. Relative to this matrix, furthermore, a verbal specification of the dots gives the same information as did the painting. (This is the principle of transmitting pictures by telegraph.) And of course two verbal accounts can give the information in very different phrasing; one of them might give the information by saying which positions are white instead of black.

Sameness of information thus stands forth clear against a pre-assigned matrix of black and white alternatives. But a trouble with trying to equate sentences in real life, in respect of the information they convey, is that no matrix of alternatives is given; we do not know what to count. There is no evident rule for separating the information from stylistic or other immaterial features of the sentences. The question when to say that two sentences mean the same proposition is consequently not adequately answered by alluding to sameness of objective information. This only rephrases the problem.

Ideally, physics does offer a matrix of alternatives and therewith an absolute concept of objective information. Two sentences agree in objective information, and so express the same proposition, when every cosmic distribution of microphysical states over space–time that would make either sentence true would make the other true as well. Each such distribution may be called a possible world, and then two sentences mean the same proposition when they are true in all the same possible worlds. The truths of pure mathematics and logic stand at an extreme, true in all possible worlds. The class of all possible worlds in which a sentence comes out true is, we might say, the sentence's objective information—indeed, its proposition. But still this idea affords us no general way of equating sentences in real life. In many cases we can clearly see that the sentences would hold under all the same distributions of microphysical states, and in many cases we can clearly see that they would not; but in the case of sentences about purposes, motives, beliefs, or aesthetic values we would scarcely know where to begin.

A different way of reckoning objective information is suggested by the empiricist tradition in epistemology. Say what difference the truth or falsity of a sentence would make to possible experience, and you have said all there is to say about the meaning of the sentence; such, in substantially the words of C. S. Peirce, is the verification theory of meaning. This theory can be seen still as identifying the proposition or meaning of a sentence with the information conveyed; but the matrix of alternatives to be used in defining information is now the totality of possible distinctions and combinations of sensory input. Some epistemologists would catalog these alternatives by introspection of sense data. Others, more naturalistically inclined, would look to neural stimulation; the organism's triggered nerve endings are the analogues of the halftone's black dots. Either way, however, a doctrine of propositions as empirical meanings runs into trouble. The trouble comes, as we shall now see, in trying to distribute the sensory evidence over separate sentences.

Diffuseness of empirical meaning   Suppose an experiment has yielded a result contrary to a theory currently held in some natural science. The theory comprises a whole bundle of conjoint hypotheses, or is resoluble into such a bundle. The most that the experiment shows is that at least one of those hypotheses is false; it does not show which. It is only the theory as a whole, and not any one of the hypotheses, that admits of evidence or counter-evidence in observation and experiment.

And how wide is a theory? No part of science is quite isolated from the rest. Parts as disparate as you please may be expected to share laws of logic and arithmetic, anyway, and to share various common-sense generalities about bodies in motion. Legalistically, one could claim that evidence counts always for or against the total system, however loose-knit, of science. Evidence against the system is not evidence against any one sentence rather than another, but can be acted on rather by any of various adjustments.

An important exception suggests itself: surely an observation is evidence for the sentence that reports that very observation, and against the sentence that predicted the contrary. Our legalist can stand his ground even here, pointing out that in an extreme case, where beliefs that have been supported overwhelmingly from time immemorial are suddenly challenged by a single contrary observation, the observation will be dismissed as illusion. What is more important, however, is that usually observation sentences are indeed individually responsive to observation. This is what distinguishes observation sentences from theoretical sentences. It is only through the responsiveness of observation sentences individually to observation, and through the connections in turn of theoretical sentences to observation sentences, that a scientific theory admits of evidence at all.

Why certain sentences are thus individually responsive to observations becomes evident when we think about how we learn language. Many expressions, including most of our earliest, are learned *ostensively*; they are learned in the situation that they describe, or in the presence of the things that they describe. They are conditioned, in short, to observations; and to publicly shared observations, since both teacher and learner have to see the appropriateness of the occasion. Now if an expression is learned in this way by everyone, everyone will tend uniformly to apply it in the presence of the same stimulations. This uniformity affords, indeed, a behavioral criterion of what to count as an observation sentence. It is because of this uniformity, also, that scientists who are checking one another's evidence gravitate to observation sentences as a point where concurrence is assured.

We learn further expressions contextually in ways that generate a fabric of sentences, complexly interconnected. The connections are such as to incline us to affirm or deny some of these sentences when inclined to affirm or deny others. These are the connections through which a theory of nature imbibes its empirical substance from the observation sentences. They are also the connections whereby, in an extremity, our theory of nature may tempt us to ignore or disavow an observation, though it would be regrettable to yield often to this temptation.

The hopelessness of distributing empirical information generally over separate sentences, or even over fairly large bundles of sentences, is in some sense widely recognized, if only by implication. For, look at it this way. It will be widely agreed that our theory of nature is under-determined by our data; and not only by the observations we actually have made and will make, but even by all the unobserved events that are of an observable kind. Briefly, our theory of nature is under-determined by all "possible" observations. This means that there can be a set H of hypotheses, and an alternative set H' incompatible with H, and it can happen that when our total theory T is changed to the extent of putting H' for H in it, the resulting theory T' still fits all possible observations just as well as T did. Evidently then H and H' convey the same empirical information, as

far as empirical information can be apportioned to H and H' at all;
but still they are incompatible. This reflection should scotch any
general notion of propositions as empirical meanings of sentences.

Why then is the notion so stubborn? Partly because the separate
sentences of science and common sense do in practice seem after all
to carry their separate empirical meanings. This is misleading, and
explicable. Thus suppose that from a combined dozen of our theoretical beliefs a scientist derives a prediction in molecular biology, and
the prediction fails. He is apt to scrutinize for possible revision
only the half dozen beliefs that belonged to molecular biology
rather than tamper with the more general half dozen having to do
with logic and arithmetic and the gross behavior of bodies. This
is a reasonable strategy—a maxim of minimum mutilation. But an
effect of it is that the portion of theory to which the discovered
failure of prediction is relevant seems narrower than it otherwise
might.

Probably, moreover, he will not even confront the six beliefs
from molecular biology impartially with the failure of prediction; he
will concentrate on one of the six, which was more suspect than the
rest. Scientists are indeed forever devising experiments for the express purpose of testing single hypotheses; and this is reasonable,
insofar as one hypothesis has been fixed upon as more tentative and
suspect than other parts of the theory.

It would be a mistake, however, to see the scientist's move as
one of questioning a single hypothesis while keeping *all* else fixed.
His experiment is prompted by suspicion of one hypothesis, yes;
and if the test proves negative he is resolved to reject that hypothesis,
but not quite it alone. Along with 'it he will reject also any which,
as he says, imply it. I must not myself now lean on a notion of
implication, for I am challenging that notion (or the associated
notion of equivalence, which is simply mutual implication). But we
do have to recognize that sentences are interconnected by means of
associations entrenched in behavior. There are the complex inter-
connections lately remarked upon: connections of varying strengths
that incline us to affirm or deny some sentences when affirming or
denying others. Whoever rejects one hypothesis will be led by these
habit patterns to reject other sentences with it.

The scientist's strategy of dividing and conquering serves
science well, but it does not show how to allocate separate empirical
evidence to separate sentences. We can allocate separate evidence to
each observation sentence, but that is about the end of it.

The uncritical acceptance of propositions as meanings of sentences is one manifestation of a widespread myth of meaning. It is as if there were a gallery of ideas, and each idea were tagged with the expression that means it; each proposition, in particular, with an appropriate sentence. In criticism of this attitude I have been airing the problem of individuation of propositions. In this connection a passing attraction of an empirical theory of meaning was the fairly clear individuation enjoyed by the domain of sensory evidence. However, we have since been finding reason to despair of this line.

The question how to individuate propositions is the question how to define equivalence of sentences—if not empirical equivalence, at any rate "cognitive" equivalence geared somehow to truth conditions. It may be well now to note and reject another inviting idea in this direction, an idea other than empirical equivalence, just to enhance our appreciation of the problem. We can define, it would seem, a strong synonymy relation for single words simply by requiring that they be interchangeable *salva veritate*. That is, putting the one word for the other always preserves the truth value of the context, turning truths into truths and falsehoods into falsehoods. More generally a word and a phrase, for example, 'bachelor' and 'unmarried man', would be called synonymous when always interchangeable *salva veritate*. Afterward we could turn about and call two sentences equivalent, in a strong sense, when they are built up of corresponding parts which are pairwise synonymous in the above sense.

Here, evidently, is a tricky way of promoting a weak relation, mere sameness of truth value, into a strong equivalence relation by sheer force of numbers. The equivalent sentences are parallel structures whose corresponding parts are related each to each by the strong relation of being interchangeable *salva veritate* in *all* sentences. The equivalence relation thus obtained has the drawback of requiring parallel structure; but this limitation can be eased somewhat by listing also some allowable grammatical transformations.

Let us now think critically about the synonymy of words to words and phrases. Consider the terms 'creature with a heart', briefly 'cordate',[1] and 'creature with kidneys', briefly 'renate'. All four terms are true of just the same creatures, but still of course we should not like to call them synonymous. They invite the title of synonymy only in pairs, 'cordate' with 'creature with a heart' and

---

[1] Not to be confused with 'chordate'.

'renate' with 'creature with kidneys'. Now how, in these cases, does our contemplated definition of synonymy fare—namely, interchangeability *salva veritate*? Can we show interchangeability of 'cordate' with 'creature with a heart', and yet failure of interchangeability of 'cordate' with 'renate'?

Perhaps we can, perhaps not; it all depends on what resources of contextual material we suppose to be available elsewhere in our language. If, for instance, the context:

(1) Necessarily all cordates are cordates

is available in the language, then the desired contrast seems to work out. Interchangeability of 'cordate' with 'renate' fails, as desired; for, putting 'renates' for the second occurrence of 'cordates' in the true sentence (1), we get a falsehood. At the same time, as desired, 'cordate' remains interchangeable with 'creature with a heart', at least in the example (1); for necessarily all cordates, by definition, have hearts.

But this successful contrast depends oddly on the resources of the language. If the adverb 'necessarily' had not been available, and in such a sense as to fail for 'all cordates are renates' and hold for 'all cordates have hearts', then this particular contrast between synonymy and failure of synonymy would have been denied us. And the unsatisfactory thing about this dependence is that the adverb 'necessarily', in the needed sense, is exactly as obscure as the notions of synonymy and equivalence that we are trying in the end to justify. If we had been content with this adverb, we could have defined equivalence in a moment: sentences are equivalent if, necessarily, they are either both true or both false.

True, other examples could be cited. The example:

(2) Tom thinks all cordates are cordates

serves as well as (1), since Tom might well not think that all cordates are renates, while still recognizing that all cordates have hearts. And (2) has the advantage of being couched in more innocent language than (1) with its cooked-up sense of necessity. However, innocence is one thing, clarity another. The 'thinks' idiom in (2), for all its ordinariness, is heir to all the obscurities of the notions of synonymy and equivalence and more.

Anyway, the 'thinks' idiom can scarcely be said to be more ordinary than the notion of equivalence. It is not as though equivalence were a new and technical notion, needing still to be paraphrased into ordinary language. On the contrary, the term is itself ordinary, for all its obscurity. The idea of equivalence, "cognitive" equivalence, seems to make sense as it stands, until scrutinized. It is only mutual implication, after all, and implication is only deducibility. The complaint against these notions is not lack of familiarity, but lack of clarity.

Are all these notions to be dispensed with in serious science? In large part I think they are. Early in Chapter 4 I shall examine and defend certain narrowly logical notions of equivalence and deducibility. Also there are relativized usages that account for much of the everyday utility of these terms; we speak of equivalence or deducibility relative to one or another tacitly accepted corpus of background information. But none of those uses, of which fair sense can be made, is of any evident avail in individuating propositions.

The doctrine of propositions seems in a way futile on the face of it, even if we imagine the individuation problem solved. For, that solution would consist in some suitable definition of equivalence of sentences; why not then just talk of sentences and equivalence and let the propositions go? The long and short of it is that propositions have been projected as shadows of sentences, if I may transplant a figure of Wittgenstein's. At best they will give us nothing the sentences will not give. Their promise of more is mainly due to our uncritically assuming for them an individuation which matches no equivalence between sentences that we see how to define. The shadows have favored wishful thinking.

Truth and semantic ascent   Philosophers who favor propositions have said that propositions are needed because truth is intelligible only of propositions, not of sentences. An unsympathetic answer is that we can explain truth of sentences to the propositionalist in his own terms: sentences are true whose meanings are true propositions. Any failure of intelligibility here is already his own fault.

But there is a deeper and vaguer reason for his feeling that truth is intelligible primarily for propositions. It is that truth should hinge on reality, not language; sentences are language. His way of producing a reality for truth to hinge on is shabby, certainly: an imaginary projection from sentences. But he is right that truth should hinge on reality, and it does. No sentence is true but reality makes it so. The sentence 'Snow is white' is true, as Tarski has taught us, if and only if real snow is really white. The same can be said of the sentence 'Der Schnee ist weiss'; language is not the point.

In speaking of the truth of a given sentence there is only indirection; we do better simply to say the sentence and so speak not about language but about the world. So long as we are speaking only of the truth of singly given sentences, the perfect theory of truth is what Wilfrid Sellars has called the disappearance theory of truth.

Truth hinges on reality; but to object, on this score, to calling sentences true, is a confusion. Where the truth predicate has its utility is in just those places where, though still concerned with reality, we are impelled by certain technical complications to mention sentences. Here the truth predicate serves, as it were, to point through the sentence to the reality; it serves as a reminder that though sentences are mentioned, reality is still the whole point.

What, then, are the places where, though still concerned with unlinguistic reality, we are moved to proceed indirectly and talk of sentences? The important places of this kind are places where we are seeking generality, and seeking it along certain oblique planes that we cannot sweep out by generalizing over objects.

We can generalize on 'Tom is mortal', 'Dick is mortal', and so on, without talking of truth or of sentences; we can say 'All men are mortal'. We can generalize similarly on 'Tom is Tom', 'Dick is Dick', '0 is 0', and so on, saying 'Everything is itself'. When on the other hand we want to generalize on 'Tom is mortal or Tom is not mortal', 'Snow is white or snow is not white', and so on, we ascend to talk of truth and of sentences, saying 'Every sentence of the form 'p or not p' is true', or 'Every alternation of a sentence with its negation is true'. What prompts this semantic ascent is not that 'Tom is mortal or Tom is not mortal' is somehow about sentences while 'Tom is mortal' and 'Tom is Tom' are about Tom. All three are about Tom. We ascend only because of the oblique way in which the instances over which we are generalizing are related to one another.

We were able to phrase our generalization 'Everything is itself' without such ascent just because the changes that were rung in passing from instance to instance—'Tom is Tom', 'Dick is Dick', '0 is 0'—were changes in names. Similarly for 'All men are mortal'. This generalization may be read 'x is mortal for all *men* x'—all things x of the sort that 'Tom' is a name of. But what would be a parallel reading of the generalization of 'Tom is mortal or Tom is not mortal'? It would read 'p or not p for all things p of the sort that sentences are names of'. But sentences are not names, and this reading is simply incoherent; it uses 'p' both in positions that call for sentence clauses and in a position that calls for a noun substantive. So, to gain our desired generality, we go up one step and talk about sentences: 'Every *sentence* of the *form* '*p* or not *p*' is *true*'.

The incoherent alternative reading might of course be expressly accorded meaning, if there were anything to gain by so doing. One could cause sentences to double as names, by specifying what they were to be names of. One might declare them to be names of propositions. In earlier pages, when propositions were still under advisement, I represented propositions as the meanings of sentences rather than as things named by sentences; still one could declare them to be named by sentences, and some there are who have done so. Until such a line is adopted, the letter '*p*' is no variable ranging over objects; it is only a schematic letter for sentences, only a dummy to mark a position appropriate to a component sentence in some logical form or grammatical construction. Once the sentences are taken as names of propositions, on the other hand, the letter '*p*' comes to double as a variable ranging over objects which are propositions. Thereafter we can coherently say '*p* or not *p* for all propositions *p*'.

However, this move has the drawback of reinstating propositions, which we saw reason not to welcome. Moreover, the move brings no visible benefit; for we already saw how to express generalizations of the desired sort without appeal to propositions, by just going up a step and attributing truth to sentences. This ascent to a linguistic plane of reference is only a momentary retreat from the world, for the utility of the truth predicate is precisely the cancellation of linguistic reference. The truth predicate is a reminder that, despite a technical ascent to talk of sentences, our eye is on the world. This cancellatory force of the truth predicate is explicit in Tarski's paradigm:

'Snow is white' is true if and only if snow is white.

Quotation marks make all the difference between talking about words and talking about snow. The quotation is a name of a sentence that contains a name, namely 'snow', of snow. By calling the sentence true, we call snow white. The truth predicate is a device of disquotation. We may affirm the single sentence by just uttering it, unaided by quotation or by the truth predicate; but if we want to affirm some infinite lot of sentences that we can demarcate only by talking about the sentences, then the truth predicate has its use. We need it to restore the effect of objective reference when for the sake of some generalization we have resorted to semantic ascent.

Tarski's paradigm cannot be generalized to read:

$$\text{`}p\text{' is true if and only if } p,$$

since quoting the schematic sentence letter '*p*' produces a name only of the sixteenth letter of the alphabet, and no generality over sentences. The truth predicate in its general use, attachable to a quantifiable variable in the fashion '*x* is true', is eliminable by no facile paradigm. It can be defined, Tarski shows, in a devious way, but only if some powerful apparatus is available. We shall see how in Chapter 3.

Tokens and eternal sentences   Having now recognized in a general way that what are true are sentences, we must turn to certain refinements. What are best seen as primarily true or false are not sentences but events of utterance. If a man utters the words 'It is raining' in the rain, or the words 'I am hungry' while hungry, his verbal performance counts as true. Obviously one utterance of a sentence may be true and another utterance of the same sentence be false.

Derivatively, we often speak also of inscriptions as true or false. Just as a sentence may admit of both a true and a false utterance, so also it may admit of both a true and a false inscription. An inscription of the sentence 'You owe me ten dollars' may be true or false depending on who writes it, whom he addresses it, to, and when.

We speak yet more derivatively when we speak of sentences outright as true or false. This usage works all right for *eternal* sentences: sentences that stay forever true, or forever false, independently of any special circumstances under which they happen to be uttered or written. Under the head of eternal sentences one thinks first of the sentences of arithmetic, since time and place are so conspicuously irrelevant to the subject matter of arithmetic. One thinks next of the laws of physics; for these, though occupied with the material world in a way that the laws of pure number are not, are meant to hold for all times and places. The general run of eternal sentences, however, are not so august as their name and these examples suggest. Any casual statement of inconsequential fact can be filled out into an eternal sentence by supplying names and dates and cancelling the tenses of verbs. Corresponding to 'It is raining' and 'You owe me ten dollars' we have the eternal sentence 'It rains in Boston, Mass., on July 15, 1968' and 'Bernard J. Ortcutt owes W. V. Quine ten dollars on July 15, 1968', where 'rains' and 'owes' are to be thought of now as tenseless.

In Peirce's terminology, utterances and inscriptions are *tokens* of the sentence or other linguistic expression concerned; and this linguistic expression is the *type* of those utterances and inscriptions. In Frege's terminology, truth and falsity are the two *truth values*. Succinctly, then, an eternal sentence is a sentence whose tokens all have the same truth value.

Conceivably, by an extraordinary coincidence, one and the same string of sounds or characters could serve for '2 < 5' in one language and '2 > 5' in another. When we speak of '2 < 5' as an eternal sentence, then, we must understand that we are considering it exclusively as a sentence in our language, and claiming the truth only of those of its tokens that are utterances or inscriptions produced in our linguistic community. By a less extraordinary coincidence, for that matter, an eternal sentence that was true could become false because of some semantic change occurring in the continuing evolution of our own language. Here again we must view the discrepancy as a difference between two languages: English as of one date and English as of another. The string of sounds or characters in question is, and remains, an eternal sentence of earlier English, and a true one; it just happens to do double duty as a falsehood in another language, later English.

When we call a sentence eternal, therefore, we are calling it eternal relative only to a particular language at a particular time.[1] Because of this awkward relativity there remains a theoretical advantage in assigning truth values to tokens, since in that quarter there is normally no question of choosing among languages and language stages; we are concerned simply with the language of the speaker or writer as of the time of speaking or writing. But in practice it can be convenient to talk simply of truth values of eternal sentences, tacitly understanding these as relativized to our present-day English language habits.

Let us now sum up our main conclusions. What are best regarded as true and false are not propositions but sentence tokens, or sentences if they are eternal. The desire for a non-linguistic truth vehicle comes of not appreciating that the truth predicate has precisely the purpose of reconciling the mention of linguistic forms with an interest in the objective world. This need of mentioning sentences, when interested rather in things, is merely a technical need that arises when we seek to generalize along a direction that cannot be swept out by a variable.

---

[1] This point worried L. J. Cohen, *The Diversity of Meaning* (London: Methuen, 1962), p. 232.

GRAMMAR

2

We lately noticed the law 'Every alternation of a sentence
with its negation is true'; it is called the law of excluded middle. It is an excessively simple but in other respects typical
law of logic. On the face of it, it talks about language: sentences.
We saw why it is phrased in linguistic terms: its instances differ
from one another in a manner other than simple variation of reference. The reason for the semantic ascent was not that the instances
themselves, e.g. 'Tom is mortal or Tom is not mortal', are linguistic
in subject matter, nor even that they are peculiarly beholden to language for their truth; one could still maintain that the trivial matter
of Tom's being either mortal or not mortal is due no less to pervasive
traits of nature than to the way we use our words. One could maintain this, at any rate, if one could make sense of the issue at all; but
I shall urge in Chapter 7 that there is difficulty in so doing.

We shall now examine, by way of contrast, a really linguistic
subject: one that not only, like logic, resorts to linguistic terms to
express its generalities, but also is concerned with language still in
the singular instances of its generalities. This subject is grammar.
Significantly enough, the truth predicate, so widely used in logical
generalities to offset the effects of semantic ascent and restore objective reference, has no place in grammatical generalities, at least
as they are classically conceived. Grammar is linguistic on purpose.

I shall describe the business of grammar first along classically
simple lines, postponing various qualifications. Let us picture the
grammarian as confronted by a speaking community and provided

with a modest list of *phonemes*. These are short speech units, the analogues of letters. What is required of them is just that everything said in the community be representable as a string of these phonemes, with never the same string for significantly different utterances. To show that two particular acoustically distinguishable sounds are significantly different for a speaker, and so should be reckoned to two distinct phonemes, it is sufficient to find an utterance that commands the speaker's assent before the one sound is substituted for the other and commands his dissent afterward. Settling the phonemes of a language is thus a fairly straightforward empirical enterprise, and we suppose it already completed when the grammarian moves in.

The grammarian's question is, then, what strings of phonemes belong to the language? What strings, that is, ever get uttered or could get uttered in the community as normal speech? The grammarian's job is to demarcate, formally, the class of all such strings of phonemes. Formally? This means staying within a purely mathematical theory of finite strings of phonemes. More explicitly, it means saying nothing that could not be said by means of a technical vocabulary in which, besides the usual logical particles and any desired auxiliary apparatus from pure mathematics, there are only the names of the phonemes and a symbol signifying the concatenation of phonemes.

A mere listing of strings would already be formal, but it would not suffice, since the desired strings, though finite in length, are infinite in number. So the grammarian has recourse to recursion: he specifies a *lexicon*, or list of words, together with various grammatical *constructions*, or steps that lead to compound expressions from constituent ones. His job is to devise his lexicon and his'constructions in such a way as to demarcate the desired class: the class of all the strings of phonemes that could be uttered in normal speech. The strings of phonemes obtainable from the lexicon by continued use of the construction should all be capable of occurring in normal speech; and, conversely, every string capable of occurring in normal speech should be obtainable from the lexicon by the constructions (or should at least be a fragment of a string which as a whole is obtainable from the lexicon by the constructions).

When we analyze a complex expression according to the constructions involved, we get something of the form of an inverted tree, like a genealogy. The complex expression is at the top. Below it, at the next level, are the "immediate constituents"—one or two or more—from which the complex expression was got by one application of some one construction. Below each of these constituents are its immediate constituents; and so on down. Each branch of the tree terminates downward in a word.

Chomsky has argued that English grammar is not satisfactorily accommodated in such trees of constructions alone; we want also grammatical transformations. Some compounds are best analyzed by working back and forth between different trees of construction, and transformations provide for this lateral movement. Even on these liberalized terms, grammar remains true to its purpose of formal demarcation, since each transformation needed for a particular grammar can be specified formally. However, transformations can be passed over for our purposes. The need of them does not extend to the artificial notations that are fashioned for purposes of logic; and it is the grammar of such notations that will occupy us after the next few pages.

Categories   As an aid to specifying the constructions, the lexicon is classified into grammatical *categories*. For we want to be able to specify a construction by saying what operation is to be performed upon any expression of such and such category; or perhaps what operation is to be performed upon any pair of expressions, one of this category and one of that. Since the compound expressions obtained by constructions are to be available as constituents under further constructions, we must also say what category each construction issues in.

Thus a construction is specified in this vein: take any expressions, belonging respectively to such and such categories, and combine them in such and such a distinctive way; the result will belong to such and such a category. Commonly the distinctive way of combining the constituents will be marked by the insertion of a distinctive particle; examples are 'or', 'plus', 'and', 'but'. Also there are constructions that operate on single constituents, rather than combining two or more; one such is negation, which consists in prefacing the constituent with the particle 'not'.

The constructions serve to add complex members to the categories, which had begun with word lists. A construction may even start a new category, which had no simple members; for instance, the class of sentences. The constructions, once specified, apply over and over, swelling the several categories *ad infinitum*.

The categories are what we used to call the parts of speech, though they need not preserve the traditional lines of cleavage. One of our categories might be that of singular terms. Another might be that of copulas. Another might be that of intransitive verbs. Another might be that of adjectives. One of our constructions might be that of applying 'not' to a copula to get a complex copula. Another might be that of prefixing a copula to an adjective to get a complex intransitive verb: 'is mortal', 'is not mortal'. Another might be that of joining a singular term to an intransitive verb to get a sentence: 'Tom is mortal', 'Tom is not mortal'. Another might be that of joining two sentences by an 'or' to get a sentence: 'Tom is mortal or Tom is not mortal'. What grammar tells us thus indirectly through its lexicon, categories, and constructions is not that this last sentence is true, but just that it is English.

What classes to dignify by the name of category depends on what constructions we are going to specify, and what distinctions of category will be helpful in specifying those constructions. However, such being the use of categories, we can foresee that two members of a category will tend to be grammatically interchangeable. That is, if you put one member for another in a proper sentence of the language you may change the sentence from true to false, but you will not change it to ungrammatical gibberish. To use a Scholastic expression revived by Geach, the members of a category are interchangeable *salva congruitate*. This circumstance suggests a theoretical definition of grammatical category, applicable outright to languages generally: the category of an expression is the class of all the expressions that are interchangeable with it *salva congruitate*. This notion of category was propounded by Husserl.

Any sentence remains grammatical, it would seem, when 'drive' is put for 'lane'; but the opposite substitution reduces 'I shall drive' to nonsense. Substitutability *salva congruitate* is thus not symmetrical. Grammarians have disguised these asymmetries by inventing distinctions: they treat 'drive' as either of two words, a noun or a verb, according as it stands where 'lane' could stand or not. But no such distinction is available if we take a word steadfastly as a string of phonemes. The forthright answer is just that 'drive' is in one category and 'lane' in another, since their interchangeability *salva congruitate* is incomplete. So far so good.

The criterion responds poorly, however, to further pressure. Taking 'lane' steadfastly as a string of phonemes, what are we to say of the fortuitous occurrence of 'lane' in 'plane'? No other word is interchangeable with 'lane' *salva congruitate* when such fortuitous occurrences are counted in. The categories, so defined, threaten to end up with one word apiece. Can we repair the definition by limiting the interchanges to positions where (unlike 'lane' in 'plane') the word figures as constituent of a grammatical construction? No, we are then caught in a circle; the notion of construction depends on that of category, and so cannot be used in defining it.

Immanence and transcendence

Theoretically there is no need of any definition of grammatical category, applicable to languages generally. To show why, it will be well at this point to contrast two sorts of linguistic notions: *immanent* ones, as I shall call them, and *transcendent* ones. A notion is immanent when defined for a particular language; transcendent when directed to languages generally.

For instance we would like it to make general sense, in advance of knowing some particular language, to ask whether a given string of phonemes belongs to that language. We would like to be able to state the grammarian's task, for *any* given language, as formal demarcation of the strings that belong to the language. This statement of his task calls for a *transcendent* notion of grammaticality, a transcendent notion of the relation of a string to a language to which it belongs. The transcendent notion does not itself pretend to formality; ideally it would be couched in behavioral terms, applicable in advance to any unspecified language. We have already seen a vague rendering of it: a string belongs to the language of a given community if it could be uttered in the community in normal speech. I shall return to this notion presently in a more critical vein.

An extreme example of the opposite, an *immanent* notion, is the notion of *der*-words in German grammar. This is a class of words which have the peculiarity of requiring so-called "weak inflection" of a following adjective. It would be silly to wonder regarding some other language, as yet unspecified, what its *der*-words are going to turn out to be. We specify the class of *der*-words in German formally, indeed by enumeration, as an intrinsically uninteresting aid to the major task of formally demarcating the total class of strings that belong to German. The notion of weak inflection is immanent too; we specify the weak inflections in German by enumeration, and, if we ever transfer the term 'weak inflection' to another language, we do so only by virtue of some felt family resemblance whereof no capital need be made. The relation between the two uses of the term would be little more than homonymy.

If, having started with some satisfactorily transcendent notion of grammaticality, we were to proceed to define the notion of a grammatical category simply by interchangeability *salva congruitate* in Husserl's way, then the notion of a grammatical category would likewise be transcendent. However, we saw reason to fear that categories so defined would prove too narrow to be useful. And anyway there is no need to force transcendence here. In doing the grammar of a particular language we formally demarcate the class of strings belonging to the language; and in order to implement a recursion for this purpose we formally specify certain helpful classes and certain constructions. If we call these classes grammatical categories, we are merely labeling the lot conveniently for the purpose of our grammatical enterprise in the particular language; and if we use the same phrase in connection with the grammar of another language, this is only a matter of family resemblance whereof no capital need be made. On this view there is no sense in wondering what the grammatical categories of some strange language might prove to be; the notion is immanent, like that of *der*-words.

The notion of a construction may be looked upon as immanent in the same way. So, for that matter, may the notion of a word, or, to speak more technically, a *morpheme*. The morpheme is sometimes carelessly defined as a shortest meaningful unit; and this definition would indeed make the notion of morpheme transcendent if it made sense at all. But by what criterion may strings of phonemes be counted meaningful, short of whole sentences or perhaps longer units? Or, if the morpheme is to be called meaningful on the ground of its merely contributing to the meaning of a sentence, why cannot the same be said of each mere phoneme? The notion of meaning is in too bad shape to afford a definition of morpheme. Nor is any definition needed, of a transcendent kind. Where to mark off the word divisions or morpheme divisions in a string of phonemes is just a question of the overall convenience and simplicity of the grammarian's recursive demarcation of the class of all strings belonging to the particular language. It is just a question what may more economically be listed initially as building blocks and what may more economically await construction as short compounds.

Lexicon, then, is similarly an immanent notion; for the lexicon simply comprises those words, or morphemes, that are assigned to categories. Some words are not so assigned but are treated rather as integral parts of the constructions themselves; thus 'not' and 'or', above. I shall recur to this point on page 28.

Grammarian's goal reexamined And what now of the notion of sentence: is it transcendent? What, in general, does it mean to say of a string of phonemes that it is a sentence for the language of a given community?

This may, on a generous interpretation, be taken to mean that the string not merely belongs to the language (i.e., could be uttered in the course of normal speech), but that it could be uttered between normal, unenforced silences. This notion of sentence is indeed transcendent. But it is not needed for the grammarian's task. As an aid to demarcating the class of grammatical strings, strings that could normally occur in the given language, the grammarian is apt to specify a so-called grammatical category consisting of the so-called sentences, but the specification will be formal and immanent; between the category so denominated for one language and the category so denominated for another language there need be nothing but a family resemblance, of which no capital is made. Typically the category so denominated will emerge in the next to last step of the formal grammar; and then, as a last step, the class of grammatical strings will be identified with the class of all fragments of strings of sentences. A transcendent notion, grammaticality, is in order just here at the top, to enable the grammarian to say what he is looking for.

Formality, for the transcendent notion of grammaticality, is not in point. But clarity and intelligibility are. What of our tentative formulation: "a string that could occur in normal speech"? It appeals to speech disposition, as distinct from actual behavior; but this I do not deplore. Talk of dispositions must be put up with, here as in any science. The behavior is evidence of the disposition; the disposition is a hypothetical internal condition that helps to cause the behavior. Such internal conditions may come increasingly to be understood as neurology progresses.

To speak of what "could occur in normal speech" is, nevertheless, objectionably vague. The vagueness is not to be laid to dispositional talk as such; it lies less in the 'could' than in the 'normal', or in their combination. The difficulty is highlighted by philosophers' examples of nonsense: Russell's "Quadruplicity drinks procrastination," Carnap's "This stone is thinking about Vienna." Some of us may view these sentences as false rather than meaningless, but even those who call them meaningless are apt to call them grammatical. Are they then to be said to be capable of occurring in normal speech? We begin to suspect that the notion of normality, in the relevant sense, leans on the notion of grammaticality instead of supporting it.

In fact, the grammarian exploits the vagueness of the transcendent notion of grammaticality, by trimming the notion to suit the convenience of his formal demarcation. He so fashions his recursion as to catch virtually everything that he actually hears in the community; and then the extras, such as Russell's and Carnap's examples, find their way in only because it would complicate the recursion to exclude them.

So a statement of the grammarian's purpose, by means of a satisfactorily transcendent notion of grammaticality, is not forthcoming. The grammarian's purpose is defined in part, rather, by his progress in achieving it. Or, not to speak in riddles, his purpose is just this: to demarcate formally, in a reasonably simple and natural way, a class of strings of phonemes which will include practically all observed utterances and exclude as much as practicable of what will never be heard. He will not even accommodate *quite* all of the utterances that he does observe; considerations of simplicity of his formal demarcation will persuade him to discard a few utterances as inadvertent and erroneous. This modest statement of the grammarian's vague objective is about the best I can do in a transcendent way; and it appeals to no transcendent notions more notable than the notion of an observed utterance.

Logical grammar Seeking no further for a theoretical definition of the grammarian's task, we turn now to a closer consideration of grammatical analysis in a more limited context: in application to notations of symbolic logic. Thanks to their artificiality, these notations admit of a gratifyingly simple grammar. Lexicon and constructions suffice, unaided by transformations. Grammatical categories, moreover, can be demarcated strictly on the basis of interchangeability *salva congruitate*; there is no longer the complication of ambiguities, nor of fortuitous occurrences like that of 'lane' in 'plane'.

The artificial form of notation that figures most prominently in modern logical theory has a grammar based on the following categories. There is a category of one-place predicates, or intransitive verbs; a category also of two-place predicates, or transitive verbs; a category also perhaps of three-place predicates, and so on. Besides these predicate categories, there is an infinite category of variables 'x', 'y', 'z', 'x'', 'y'', 'z'', 'x''', etc. The accent that is applied to 'x' to form 'x'', and to 'x'' to form 'x''', indicates no relation but serves merely to augment the supply of variables.

The lexicon of a language is a finite set, for the grammarian presents it as a list. We may imagine the predicates thus presented. As for the infinite category of variables, we must view it as generated from a finite lexicon by iteration of a construction. The variables in the lexicon are just the letters 'x', 'y', and 'z', and the construction is *accentuation*, the application of one accent at a time. Thus, the variable 'x'' is grammatically composite.

The rest of the grammar consists of further grammatical constructions. One of these is *predication* of a one-place predicate. It consists in joining such a predicate, perhaps the verb 'walks', and a variable to form a sentence: '*x* walks'. The result is an *atomic* sentence, in the sense of containing no subordinate sentence. Also it is an *open* sentence, because of the variable. It is true *for* certain values of the variable, namely, those that walk, and false for other values, but of itself it is neither true nor false; such is the way of an open sentence.

A further construction is the predication of a two-place predicate. It consists in joining such a predicate, say the transitive verb 'loves', and two variables, to form—again—an atomic open sentence: '*x* loves *y*'. There is also perhaps the predication of a three-place predicate, and so on. All these predication constructions join predicates with one or more variables to produce members of a new category, that of sentences. It is a category of compound expressions only; for the sentence, even when atomic, is compounded of a predicate and one or more variables.

The remaining constructions are constructions of sentences from sentences. One such construction is *negation*, which consists in prefixing the symbol '~' or 'not' to a sentence to form a sentence. One is *conjunction*, in the logical sense of the word. It consists in joining two sentences by the particle 'and', or in symbolic notation a dot, to produce a complex sentence.

Finally, there is a third construction on sentences, namely *existential quantification*. It applies to an open sentence and a variable to produce a sentence. The variable, say the letter '*x*', is put into a so-called quantifier in the manner '$\exists x$', and this quantifier is prefixed to the open sentence in the manner '$\exists x(x$ walks)'. The resulting sentence says there is something that walks.

Such, in its entirety, is the logical grammar that I wanted to present. It lacks only the list of predicates. This list could include the one-place predicates 'walks', 'is white', the two-place predicates 'loves', '$<$', 'is heavier than', 'is divisible by', and so on. The logician has no interest in completing the lexicon, for it is indifferent to the structure of the language.

Redundant devices

I would seem to have omitted not only the lexicon of predicates but also some constructions which are logical in character. One such is *alternation*, a construction that joins two sentences by the particle 'or' to form a complex sentence. This construction is useful in practice, but superfluous in theory. Every logic student knows how to paraphrase it, using only negation and conjunction. Imagining any constituent sentence in the position of the letters '*p*' and '*q*', we can paraphrase '*p* or *q*' as '∼(∼*p* . ∼*q*)'.

Another important construction that is logical in character is the *conditional*. This construction produces a compound sentence from two constituent sentences by applying the particle 'if': 'if *p*, *q*'. The sense of this familiar construction is not always clear. 'If Flora were fairer than Amy, Flora would be fair indeed'; 'If Flora were fairer than Amy, Amy would be plain indeed'. Commonly the force of a conditional is indeterminate except by reference to the purposes of some broader context. The conditional also has its clear and self-contained uses, but the services rendered by these uses can be rendered as well by negation, conjunction, and existential quantification. For example, 'If an animal has a heart, it has kidneys' is adequately paraphrased thus:

$$\sim \exists x \ (x \text{ is an animal . } x \text{ has a heart . } \sim(x \text{ has kidneys)}).$$

Often the purpose of a conditional, 'if *p*, *q*', can be served simply by negation and conjunction: ∼(*p* . ∼*q*), the so-called *material conditional*.

Along with the conditional there is the *biconditional*, formed by means of the polysyllabic particle 'if and only if'. It adds no problem, for it can be expressed by means of conjunction and the conditional: 'if *p*, *q* . if *q*, *p*'. In particular thus the *material biconditional* becomes '∼(*p* . ∼*q*) . ∼(*q* . ∼*p*)', for which I shall use the customary abbreviation '*p* ↔ *q*'.

The truth values of negations, conjunctions, alternations, and material conditionals and biconditionals are determined, obviously, by the truth values of the constituent sentences. Accordingly these constructions, and others sharing this trait, are called *truth functions*. It is well known and easily shown that all truth functions can be paraphrased into terms of negation and conjunction.

Note carefully the role of the schematic letters '*p*' and '*q*' in the above explanations. They do not belong to the *object language*—the language that I have been explaining with their help. They serve diagrammatically to mark positions where sentences of the object language are to be imagined. Similarly, the schematic notation '*Fx*' may conveniently be used diagrammatically to mark the position of a sentence when we want to direct attention to the presence therein of the variable '*x*' as a *free* or unquantified variable. Thus we depict the form of existential quantification schematically as '∃*x Fx*'. The schematic letter 'F', like 'p' and 'q', is foreign to the object language.

I explained why alternation, the conditional, and the biconditional are omitted from our list of constructions. A similar remark applies to *universal quantification:* $\forall x \; Fx$. The open sentence in the position of 'Fx' is satisfied by every object x; such is the force of '$\forall x \; Fx$'. Universal quantification is prominent in logical practice but superfluous in theory, since '$\forall x \; Fx$' obviously amounts to '$\sim\!\exists x \sim\! Fx$'.

Another frill that I have dispensed with is the admission of distinct categories of variables, to range over distinct sorts of objects. This again is a mere convenience, and is strictly redundant. Instead of admitting a new style of variables 'α', 'β', etc., to range over some new sort K of objects, we can just let the old variables range over the old and new objects indiscriminately and then adopt a predicate 'K' to mark off the new objects when desired. Then instead of the special style of quantification '$\exists \alpha \; F\alpha$' we can write in the old style '$\exists x \; (Kx \, . \, Fx)$'.

Names and functors Chief among the omitted frills is the *name*. This again is a mere convenience and strictly redundant, for the following reason. Think of 'a' as a name, and think of 'Fa' as any sentence containing it. But clearly 'Fa' is equivalent to '$\exists x \; (a = x \, . \, Fx)$'. We see from this consideration that 'a' needs never occur except in the context '$a =$'. But we can as well render '$a =$' always as a simple predicate 'A', thus abandoning the name 'a'. 'Fa' gives way thus to '$\exists x \; (Ax \, . \, Fx)$', where the predicate '$A$' is true solely of the object a.

It may be objected that this paraphrase deprives us of an assurance of uniqueness that the name has afforded. It is understood that the name applies to only one object, whereas the predicate 'A' supposes no such condition. However, we lose nothing by this, since we can always stipulate by further sentences, when we wish, that 'A' is true of one and only one thing:

$$\exists x \; Ax, \qquad \sim\!\exists x \; \exists y \; (Ax \, . \, Ay \, . \, \sim\!(x = y) \,).$$

(The identity sign '$=$' here would either count as one of the simple predicates of the language or be paraphrased in terms of them.)

The notation without names talks still of a and other objects, for they are the values of the quantified variables. An object can also be specified uniquely, still, by presenting some open sentence (in one variable) which that object uniquely satisfies. 'Ax' is such a sentence for the object a. And the names can even be restored at pleasure, as a convenient redundancy, by a convention of abbreviation. This convention would be simply the converse of the procedure by which we just now eliminated names. Each predication, let us say '*Fa*', containing the name '*a*', would be explained as an abbreviation of the quantification '∃*x* (A*x* . F*x*)'. In effect this is somewhat the idea behind Russell's theory of singular descriptions.

In the redundant system that retains names, there are two categories of singular terms: the variables and the names. The categories count as two because names cannot stand in quantifiers. The asymmetry illustrated by 'drive' and 'lane' above recurs thus in this artificial setting: you can put a variable for a name *salva congruitate* but not always vice versa.

Names are convenient, as are universal quantifiers and the excess truth-function signs. In practice we use them all, and more: there are also the *functors*. A one-place functor, e.g. 'square of' or 'father of', attaches to a singular term to yield a singular term. A two-place functor, e.g. '+', joins two singular terms to yield a singular term. Correspondingly for three and more places. The functors, again, are just convenient redundancy; they can all be dropped in favor of appropriate predicates, by an extension of the method by which we dropped names.

Functors generate complex singular terms. These and names belong in a single category—the category of singular terms other than variables. The complex singular terms may contain variables; but what sets the variable itself apart from all these other singular terms is its occurrence in quantifiers.

Artificial languages of the forms we have been considering may, following Tarski, be called *standard*. This term is used for those that admit names, complex singular terms, functors, and the lesser devices lately noted, as well as for those that do not. These last, the standard languages of the simple and austere sort, differ from one another only in their vocabulary of predicates. They share the variables, predication, negation, conjunction, and existential quantification.

Lexicon, particle, and name The grammatical pattern of category and construction brings out a distinction, customary in linguistics, between two kinds of vocabulary: the lexicon and the particles. It is not a new distinction. It has long governed Japanese orthography, which uses a special Japanese syllabary for the particles (and another for European loan words) but preserves Chinese characters for the lexicon.

The distinction is this: the words classed in the categories comprise the lexicon, whereas the words or signs that are not thus classified but are handled only as parts of specific constructions are the particles. In our logical notation, thus, one particle is the sign '~' whose prefixture constitutes the negation construction; another is the dot, whose interposition constitutes the conjunction construction; another is the accent, whose application constitutes the variable-generating construction; another is the sign 'Ǝ' of the quantification construction; and others are the parentheses, used in the quantification construction and sometimes also, for grouping, in negation and conjunction.

The distinction between lexicon and particles is yet more venerable in the West than in the East. It is identifiable with the Scholastic distinction between categorematic and syncategorematic words. This, even in its terminology, goes back to antiquity.[1] There is a connection with categorical propositions in the logic of the syllogism; the terms in a categorical proposition are categorematic.

The terminology seems curiously pat now, given the modern notion of grammatical category; for the categorematic expressions are the members of categories. But the theory of grammatical categories, lexicon, and constructions does not hark back thus. The definition of 'categorematic' was apt to be something lame like 'significative in itself'. Still our notion of lexicon, or of what goes into the grammatical categories, seems to capture the feeling.

Being in the lexicon does not, of course, mean being a name. If an occasional Scholastic or modern philosopher seems to identify the distinction between categorematic and syncategorematic with the distinction between names and other words, it is easy to see why he might: he has already taken the previous step of construing predicates as names of attributes. The terminology can in this way change, so that a philosopher who wants to deny that predicates are names finally does so by calling them syncategorematic.

The old terms 'categorematic' and 'syncategorematic' are a curiosity that I shall put aside. But I must reiterate the antecedent point, which squarely concerns our present business: being in the lexicon does not mean being a name. Taking predicates as lexical does not mean taking predicates as names and accordingly positing attributes for the predicates to be names of. What distinguishes a name is that it can stand coherently in the place of a variable, in predication, and will yield true results when used to instantiate true universal quantifications. Predicates are not names; predicates are the

---

[1] See Norman Kretzmann, "Syncategorematic," *The Encyclopedia of Philosophy* (New York: Macmillan, 1967), VII, 373.

other parties to predication. Predicates and singular terms are what predication joins.

I deny that predicates are names without having to deny that there are such things as attributes. That is a separate question. We can admit attributes by reckoning them to the universe of objects which are the values of our variables of quantification. We can name them, too, if we allow names in our language; but these names will not be predicates. They will be singular terms, substitutable for variables; abstract singular terms like 'whiteness' or 'walking', not predicates like 'is white' or 'walks'.

There are those who use so-called predicate variables in predicate position and in quantifiers, writing things like '∃F Fx'. The values of these variables are attributes; the constants substitutable for the variables are, we are told, predicates; so that predicates double as names of attributes. My complaint is that questions of existence and reference are slurred over through failure to mark distinctions. Predicates are wanted in all sentences regardless of whether there are attributes to refer to, and the dummy predicate 'F' is wanted generally for expository purposes without thought of its being a quantifiable variable taking attributes as values. If we are also going to quantify over attributes and refer to them, then clarity is served by using recognizable variables and distinctive names for the purpose and not mixing these up with the predicates.

Criterion of lexicon   The distinction between lexicon and particles is not, I have twice said, a distinction between names and other words. Let us now go back and examine it more closely for what it is. How do we settle what words to sort into categories, and hence consign to the lexicon, and what words to absorb as particles into the constructions? Consider the negative sentence '~(x walks)', as of our logical grammar. I have reckoned 'x' and 'walks' to the lexicon, while calling '~' a mere particle incidental to the negation construction. The whole sentence is constructed by negation from the constituent sentence 'x walks', which is constructed by predication from the lexical words 'x' and 'walks'. Why not, instead, treat 'walks' as a particle on a par with '~'? This would mean skipping any general predication construction and recognizing instead a walking construction, along with the negation construction. On this view, 'x walks' is got from the single lexical word 'x' by the walking construction and '~(x walks)' is then got from 'x walks' by the negation construction. Why not? Or, taking the other turning, why not treat '~' as lexical along with 'x' and 'walks'? This would mean recognizing a construction which, applied to the lexical word '$\sim$' and a sentence 'x walks', yields a sentence '$\sim(x$ walks$)$'. Or we could recognize a three-place construction leading directly from three lexical words '$\sim$', 'x', and 'walks' to '$\sim(x$ walks$)$'.

The choice among these alternatives of grammatical theory turns upon considerations of the following kind. By iteration of constructions, complex expressions accrete *ad infinitum;* and we must have infinitely expansible categories to receive them. Now a reason for reckoning a word to the lexicon is that it gets into one of these big categories through being interchangeable *salva congruitate* with the other expressions in the category.

What, then, about the words that do not get into big categories? Each such word is in a class fairly nearly by itself; few words are interchangeable with it *salva congruitate*. Instead of listing a construction applicable to such a word and to few if any others, we simply count the word an integral part of the construction itself. Such is the status of particles.

Thus take first the three variables 'x', 'y', 'z'. They are in the lexicon because the variables make up a category, being infinite in number. If we could make do with the three variables 'x', 'y', 'z' to the exclusion of their unending accented suite, then we would drop variables as a category and demote variables from the status of lexicon to the status of particles. Instead of the construction which was the predication of a one-place predicate, we would thereupon recognize three constructions: attachment of 'x', of 'y', and of 'z'. Instead of the construction which was the predication of a two-place predicate, we would recognize nine constructions: attachment of 'xx', of 'xy', . . . , and of 'zz'. Instead of existential quantification we would recognize three constructions: prefixture of '$\exists x$', of '$\exists y$', and of '$\exists z$'.

I have not said which particular predicates are to be present in the language—whether 'walks', 'is red', 'is heavier than', 'is divisible by', etc.; for the point is indifferent to the logical structure of the language. This studied indefiniteness, indeed, and not infinitude, is the main reason for counting predicates as lexical rather than as particles. For note that I have not been recognizing any predicate-yielding constructions. The list of predicates is meant to be finite and fixed, but merely different for each particular language of the contemplated kind. For each such language, with its predicates listed, we could demote predicates to the status of particles and recognize a distinct construction corresponding to each—as we lately contemplated for 'walks'.

The indefiniteness of the supply of predicates is not the only reason for counting the predicates as lexical. One may wish also to leave the way open for some predicate-yielding construction that would generate an infinitude of complex predicates.

It is worth remarking that if one chooses to admit predicate-yielding constructions and exploits them to the full, he can even make some such constructions do the work of the quantifiers and variables themselves. There are a half-dozen such constructions which, in combination, would enable us to drop variables and quantifiers altogether. One of the constructions is the negating of a predicate; one is the active-passive transformation that turns the two-place predicate 'loves' into 'is loved by'; and there are four others.[1] But this is a drastic alternative to standard logical grammar.

Time, events, adverbs Our standard logical grammar is conspicuously untouched by the complications of *tense* which so dominate European languages. Logical grammar, like modern physics, is best served by treating time as a dimension coordinate with the spatial dimensions; treating date, in other words, as just another determinable on a par with position. Verbs can then be taken as tenseless. Temporal predicates, such as the two-place predicate 'is earlier than', belong in the lexicon on a par merely with predicates of position or color or anything else. Any temporal details that we may want to include in a sentence, in the absence of tensed verbs, we may add explicitly in the same way that we might add details of position or color.

A body is thus visualized eternally as a four-dimensional whole, extending up and down, north and south, east and west, hence and ago. A shrinking body is seen as tapered toward the hence; a growing body is tapered toward the ago.

We might think of a *physical object*, more generally and generously, as simply the whole four-dimensional material content, however sporadic and heterogeneous, of some portion of space-time. Then if such a physical object happens to be fairly firm and coherent internally, but coheres only rather slightly and irregularly with its spatio-temporal surroundings, we are apt to call it a body. Other physical objects may be spoken of more naturally as processes, happenings, events. Still others invite no distinctive epithet.

This four-dimensional view of things is an aid to relativity physics; also it is a simplification of grammar, by resolution of tense; but either of these characterizations understates its importance for logic.

[1] See my *Methods of Logic*, 4th ed. (Cambridge: Harvard, 1982), § 45.

Think how awkward it is, without some such view, to make sense of applying a predicate to something that no longer exists; or to make sense of quantifying over objects that never coexisted at any one time, and assembling such objects into sets.

I have stressed how much our austere little standard grammar potentially encompasses. Its lack of tense, its lack even of names and all complex singular terms, detract none from its adequacy. Still I cannot claim that it is adequate to all purposes of cognitive discourse: that everything can be said in a language comprising just these constructions and variables and a finite lexicon of predicates.

There is for instance the question, raised by Davidson, of adverbs. If all predicates are to be simple, there can be no provision for adverbial modification of predicates to form new predicates. We might therefore be moved to liberalize our grammar by recognizing some supplementary predicate-yielding constructions, capable of generating complex predicates in infinite supply. Any fixed and finite lot of adverbs could be accommodated in this way, each as a particle marking a separate predicate-yielding construction. But more is wanted: adverbs themselves—adverbial phrases—are evidently wanted in unending supply and without limit of complexity. For this purpose, grammatical categories of adverbs are required; also constructions for adjoining adverbs to predicates. Such a development would be, it seems, a genuine and not just stylistic extension of our standard logical grammar.

Or can we hope still to achieve all these adverbial ends by other means? Perhaps if we were just to add to the lexicon some cunningly construed new predicates, and add to the range of values of the quantified variables some peculiarly helpful new domain of objects, we would achieve all those adverbial ends without bursting the bonds of our standard grammar. Davidson, exploring this possibility, sees *events* as the helpful new domain of objects. He might analyze 'x walks rapidly (sometime or other)' somewhat as '$\exists y$ (y is a walking of x . y is rapid)'. The troublesome adverb 'rapidly' has given way here to an innocuous predicate, 'is rapid'. The one-place predicate 'walks', or better the two-place predicate of walking at a time, has given way to a different two-place predicate, relating the walking event to the walker. The relevant values of 'y' are events.

But it is not yet clear whether we can make do here with events in the weak and innocent sense noted early in this section, under the head of physical objects. So construed, no two events have the same spatio-temporal boundaries. If events in some other sense are required, we shall have to face the problem of how to individuate them. It was inadequacy of individuation, after all, that turned us against propositions in Chapter 1.

However this interesting venture may turn out, there are other challenges to the adequacy of our standard grammar. We must reckon somehow with the stubborn idioms of *propositional attitude*—'thinks that', 'believes that', 'wishes that', 'strives that', and the rest. These cause sentences to be constituents of constructions other than truth functions and quantification.

There are several ways of organizing these matters. One way is to recognize a construction that builds a name from a sentence by prefixing the particle 'that'. This means restoring names as a grammatical category. Also it raises the question what sort of things 'that'-clauses name: perhaps propositions, so dimly viewed in Chapter 1? Also it raises the question of having to subdivide the category of two-place predicates, since some of them ('thinks', 'believes', 'wishes', 'strives') can apply to a 'that'-clause while others ('eats', '>') cannot. This, however, is easily settled by just regarding sentences of the form 'x eats that p' and '$x > $ that p' as trivially false rather than meaningless. One sees in this latter expedient, by the way, an illustration of what was remarked upon earlier in this chapter in connection with 'Quadruplicity drinks procrastination' and 'This stone is thinking about Vienna'; an illustration, namely, of how grammatical simplicity can be gained by taking grammaticality broadly. By counting 'x eats that p' grammatical we make do with one category of two-place predicates in place of two.

Such, then, is one way of arranging the grammar of propositional attitudes: by recognizing a construction that builds a singular term from a sentence by prefixing the particle 'that'. Now an obvious second way is to recognize, instead, a construction that builds a one-place predicate from a two-place predicate and a sentence by interposing the particle 'that'. This way has the advantage of not involving names of propositions. It does not dispense with propositions themselves, however, or whatever the objects of propositional attitudes might be presumed to be; for, in taking 'believes' and the rest as two-place predicates it still admits 'x believes y' and the like.

A third way is to treat 'believes that' and the rest as comprising a new lexical category, the *attitudinatives*, and then to recognize a construction that builds a one-place predicate such as 'believes that Darwin erred' by concatenating an attitudinative 'believes that' and a sentence 'Darwin erred'. On this analysis 'thinks', 'believes', etc., are not cast with 'eats' and '$>$'; they are not predicates at all. On this analysis, objects of propositional attitudes are no longer called for. But there is a price: one can no longer say 'x believes y', and the like, with quantifiable 'y'. One can no longer say that there is something that x believes.

Besides the idioms of propositional attitude there are those of *modality*: 'necessarily', 'possibly'. These again cause sentences to be constituents of constructions other than truth functions and quantification. To accommodate them we could recognize a necessity construction that forms a sentence from a sentence by prefixing the particle 'necessarily'. As for 'possibly', it can be seen simply as a concatenation of three particles marking three successive one-place constructions: 'not necessarily not'.

The idioms both of propositional attitude and of modality are notoriously unclear from a logical and philosophical point of view. Their want of clarity was remarked on in Chapter 1, but it is yet more abject than there indicated. Troubles can arise, in such contexts, from putting one side of a true statement of identity for the other. The sentence:

Tom thinks that Tully wrote the *Ars Magna*

may be true, and yet become false when 'Cicero' is put for 'Tully', even though Cicero = Tully. Questions consequently arise regarding the coherence of using a neutral variable of quantification in such a position:

Tom believes that x wrote the *Ars Magna*.

If this open sentence is going to have to be true or false of a man x depending on which of his names we refer to him by, we may question whether as an open and quantifiable sentence it makes sense at all.

This difficulty over the interpretation of open sentences and their quantifications affects modal contexts as well as the idioms of propositional attitude. On the other hand, all these idioms reduce to a pretty hollow mockery if we never quantify into them. Efforts to save the situation prove to involve us either in considerations of essence and accident and kindred dim distinctions, or else in elaborate further grammatical apparatus which I forbear to enlarge upon here.

We should be within our rights in holding that no formulation of any part of science is definitive so long as it remains couched in idioms of propositional attitude or modality. But to claim this is more modest than to claim that our standard logical grammar is enough grammar for science. Such good uses as the modalities are ever put to can probably be served in ways that are clearer and already known; but the idioms of propositional attitude have uses in which they are not easily supplanted. Let us by all means strive for clearer devices adequate to those purposes; but meanwhile we have no assurance that the new devices, once found, will fit the elegant grammar that we are calling standard.

TRUTH

3

Logicians and grammarians are alike in habitually talking about sentences. But we saw the difference. The logician talks of sentences only as a means of achieving generality along a dimension that he cannot sweep out by quantifying over objects. The truth predicate then preserves his contact with the world, where his heart is.

Between logicians and grammarians there is a yet closer bond than the shared concern with sentences. Take in particular the artificial grammar of Chapter 2, which was made for logic. The relevance of such a grammar to logic is that logic explores the truth conditions of sentences in the light of how the sentences are grammatically constructed. Logic chases truth up the tree of grammar.

In particular the logic of truth functions chases truth up through two constructions, negation and conjunction, determining the truth values of the compounds from those of the constituents. Implicitly all truth functions get this treatment, thanks to iteration.

If logic traces truth conditions through the grammatical constructions, and the truth functions are among these constructions, truth-function logic is assured. And conversely, if logic is to be centrally concerned with tracing truth conditions through the grammatical constructions, an artificial grammar designed by logicians is bound to assign the truth functions a fundamental place among its constructions. The grammar that we logicians are tendentiously calling standard is a grammar designed with no other thought than to

35

facilitate the tracing of truth conditions. And a very good thought this is.

We chose a standard grammar in which the simple sentences are got by predication, and all further sentences are generated from these by negation, conjunction, and existential quantification. Predication, in this grammar, consists always in adjoining predicates to variables and not to names. So all the simple sentences are *open* sentences, like 'x walks' and '$x > y$'; they have free variables. Consequently they are neither true nor false; they are only satisfied by certain things, or pairs of things, or triples, etc. The open sentence 'x walks' is satisfied by each walker and nothing else. The open sentence '$x > y$' is satisfied by each descending pair of numbers and no other pairs.

Already at the bottom of the tree, thus, logic's pursuit of truth conditions encounters a complication. The relevant logical trait of negation is not just that negation makes true closed sentences out of false ones and vice versa. We must add that the negation of an open sentence with one variable is satisfied by just the things that that sentence was not satisfied by; also that the negation of an open sentence with two variables is satisfied by just the pairs that that sentence was not satisfied by; and so on.

I have taken to speaking of pairs. The pairs wanted are *ordered* pairs; that is, we must distinguish the pairs $\langle x, y \rangle$ and $\langle y, x \rangle$ so long as $x \neq y$. For we have to say that the pair $\langle 3, 5 \rangle$ satisfies '$x < y$' while $\langle 5, 3 \rangle$ does not. The law of ordered pairs is that if $\langle x, y \rangle = \langle z, w \rangle$ then $x = z$ and $y = w$. Beyond that the properties of the ordered pair are of no concern. If one wants to decide just what objects the ordered pairs are to be, one can decide it quite arbitrarily as long as the above law is fulfilled. Thus we might form the set $\{x, 1\}$ whose members are x and the number 1, and form also the set $\{y, 2\}$, and then define $\langle x, y \rangle$ as the set whose members are these two sets. However, confusion ensues if x or y is itself 1 or 2. So let us start not with $\{x, 1\}$ but with $\{\{x\}, 1\}$, where $\{x\}$ is the set whose sole member is x; for, even if x is a number, $\{x\}$ presumably is not. Thus $\langle x, y \rangle$ may be defined as the set whose two members are $\{\{x\}, 1\}$ and $\{\{y\}, 2\}$.

In thus construing ordered pairs we do not assume that within the standard language under discussion—the *object language*—the values of the variables include sets, nor that they include ordered pairs in any sense. The use I propose to make of ordered pairs proceeds wholly within the *metalanguage*—the ordinary unformalized language in which I describe and discuss the object language. When

I say that the pair ⟨ 3, 5 ⟩ satisfies the sentence '*x* < *y*', I am assuming for the time being that the sentence '*x* < *y*' belongs to the object language and that the domain of objects of the object language includes the numbers 3 and 5; but I do not need to assume that this domain include their pair ⟨ 3, 5 ⟩. The pair belongs to the apparatus of my study of the object language, and this is enough.

Satisfaction of open sentences with three free variables calls for ordered triples, ⟨ *x*, *y*, *z* ⟩; and so on up. We can define ⟨ *x*, *y*, *z* ⟩ as the set whose three members are {{*x*}, 1}, {{*y*}, 2}, and {{*z*}, 3}. Correspondingly for ⟨ *x*, *y*, *z*, *w* ⟩, and so on. Also, heading the list, we get the *single* ⟨ *x* ⟩ as the set whose sole member is { {*x*}, 1}. The plan avoids confusion if no numbers are interpreted as one–member sets. Actually 1 is often interpreted as {0}; but it can be shown that this single exception still leads to no confusion.

A simpler version of ⟨ *x*, *y* ⟩, widely used, is {{*x*}, {*x*, *y*}}. Longer sequences can be defined by iteration: ⟨ *x*, *y*, *z* ⟩ as ⟨ ⟨ *x*, *y* ⟩, *z* ⟩, then ⟨ *x*, *y*, *z*, *w* ⟩ as ⟨ ⟨ *x*, *y* ⟩, *z*, *w* ⟩, and so on. But David Miller has shown me that this method leads to ambiguities of length if we admit sequences of different lengths in the same contexts, as I shall be doing.

Satisfaction by sequences   Let us refer to singles, pairs, triples, and so on collectively as *sequences*. This term will enable us to speak of the satisfaction of sentences in a briefer and more general way, by sparing us the need of considering each different number of variables separately. We may speak of a sequence as satisfying a sentence if the sentence comes out true when we take the first thing of the sequence as the value of the variable '*x*', the second thing of the sequence as the value of '*y*', and so on, ticking the variables off in alphabetical order: '*x*,' '*y*', '*z*', '*x*'', etc.

Thus take the open sentence '*x* conquered *y*'. (Strictly speaking, not to complicate our logical grammar with tense, we should think of the predicate 'conquered' as meaning, tenselessly, 'conquereth at some time'.) This open sentence is satisfied by the pair ⟨ Caesar, Gaul ⟩; for '*x*' and '*y*' are the first and second variables of the alphabet, and Caesar and Gaul are the first and second things in the pair, and Caesar conquered Gaul.

This formulation allows the length of the sequence to exceed the number of variables in the sentence. The things in the sequence corresponding to missing variables simply have no effect. For instance, the sentence '*x* conquered *y*' is satisfied by the sequence ⟨ Caesar, Gaul, *a* ⟩ for any *a*; it is only the first two places of the sequence that are relevant to '*x* conquered *y*'.

It goes naturally with this convention, moreover, to speak of any sentence simply as *true* when it is true for all values of its free variables and thus satisfied by all sequences. Thus '$x = x$' counts as true. This convention will save us some tedious clauses in subsequent pages. And let us call a sentence *false* when false for all values.

A technical question arises when a sequence is too short to reach all the variables of a sentence. The most convenient ruling is this: when a sequence has fewer than i places, define its ith element as identical with its last element—as if this were repeated over and over.* Thus the sentence '$x \leqq y$' is satisfied by the sequence $\langle 1 \rangle$, which is to say simply 1; for, it is satisfied by $\langle 1, 1 \rangle$. In addition, in view of the second paragraph back, it is satisfied by $\langle 1, 1, y \rangle$ for every choice of y.

The austerity of our standard grammar, which bans even names and functors, is a convenience insofar as we are concerned not to use a language but to talk about it. In use, names and functors are convenient. So austerity will prevail only in the object language, whose sentences 'x walks', '$x < y$', 'x conquered y', etc., I am talking about. In speaking of these austere sentences, and of what sequences satisfy them, I freely use our own conveniently less austere everyday language; hence names like 'Caesar' and 'Gaul', and compound singular terms like '$\langle$Caesar, Gaul$\rangle$'.

Still the sentences even of the object language do not all have free variables. The simple sentences do; closed simple sentences like 'Caesar conquered Gaul' are not available. But there are complex closed sentences, such as '$\exists x \, \exists y \, (x$ conquered $y)$'. So it is proper to ask, still, what sequences might be said to satisfy a closed sentence; and the answer is easy. Just as all but the first and second things in a sequence are irrelevant to 'x conquered y', so all the things in a sequence are irrelevant to a sentence devoid of free variables. Thus a closed sentence is satisfied by every sequence or none according simply as it is true or false.

This last remark applies indeed to open sentences as well as closed ones, thanks to the convention that we adopted a half page back. Every sequence satisfies every true sentence and no false one. The definition of *truth* in terms of satisfaction is easy indeed: *satisfaction by all sequences*. Satisfaction is the concept that the work goes into.

This work, to which we now turn, is due to Tarski except for minor details. It will be facilitated by our new apparatus of sequences

---

* Here I am indebted to George Boolos and James A. Thomas.

and our accompanying conventions. Turning back now to the truth functions, we can say once for all that a sequence satisfies the negation of a given sentence if and only if it does not satisfy the given sentence. Similarly a sequence satisfies a conjunction if and only if it satisfies each of the sentences. We can say these things without regard to how long the sequences are and without regard to how many free variables the sentences have, if indeed any.

There is something artificial and arbitrary, one feels, about the appeal to alphabetical order of variables. A seemingly gratuitous difference is thereby created between the open sentences 'x conquered y' and 'y conquered z'; ⟨Caesar, Gaul⟩ satisfies the one and not the other. Would we perhaps do better to appeal not to alphabetical order but to order of first appearance in the sentence? This way, ⟨Caesar, Gaul⟩ would satisfy 'x conquered y' and 'y conquered z' indifferently.

Conjunction holds the answer to this question. On our alphabetical approach, ⟨Caesar, Gaul, Brutus⟩ satisfies both 'x conquered y' and 'z killed x' and also therefore their conjunction 'x conquered y . z killed x'; all is thus in order. On the other approach, ⟨Caesar, Gaul⟩ would satisfy 'x conquered y'; ⟨Brutus, Caesar⟩ would satisfy 'z killed x'; and only a rather complicated rule of conjunction could lead us from these data to the desired conclusion, that ⟨Caesar, Gaul, Brutus⟩ satisfies 'x conquered y . z killed x'. It is alphabetical order, thus, that helps us pair up the variables across conjunctions. The difference between 'x conquered y' and 'y conquered z' is after all not gratuitous, when you think how differently they fare in conjunction with some further clause such as 'z killed x'.

We arrived at a compact statement of the satisfaction conditions of negations and conjunctions, relative to their constituents. The negation is satisfied by just the sequences that its constituent is not satisfied by, and the conjunction is satisfied by just the sequences that its constituents are both satisfied by. Now what of the remaining construction, existential quantification? An existential quantification consists of some sentence preceded by an existential quantifier whose variable is, say, the ith variable of the alphabet. This quantification, then, is satisfied by a given sequence if and only if the constituent sentence is satisfied by some sequence that matches the given one except perhaps in its ith place.

For example, take '∃y (x conquered y)'. This is satisfied by a given sequence if and only if 'x conquered y' is satisfied by a sequence that matches the given one except perhaps in second place. Thus ∃y (x conquered *y*)' is, as desired, satisfied by every sequence whose first thing is Caesar; we get this result because '*x* conquered *y*' is satisfied by every sequence whose first and second things are Caesar and Gaul.

Note how our recent device for overlong sequences figures here. '∃*y* (*x* conquered *y*)' is satisfied by Caesar, that is, ⟨Caesar⟩, and by every prolongation of ⟨Caesar⟩; and '*x* conquered *y*' is satisfied by every prolongation of ⟨Caesar, Gaul⟩.

Tarski's definition of truth   A reasonable way of explaining an expression is by saying what conditions make its various contexts true. Hence one is perhaps tempted to see the above satisfaction conditions as explaining negation, conjunction, and existential quantification. However, this view is untenable; it involves a vicious circle. The given satisfaction conditions for negation, conjunction, and quantification presuppose an understanding of the very signs they would explain, or of others to the same effect. A negation is explained as satisfied by a sequence when the constituent sentence is *not* satisfied by it; a conjunction is satisfied by a sequence when the one constituent sentence *and* the other are satisfied by it; and an existential quantification is satisfied by a sequence when the constituent sentence is satisfied by *some* suitably similar sequence. If we are prepared to avail ourselves thus of 'not', 'and', and 'some' in the course of explaining negation, conjunction, and existential quantification, why not proceed more directly and just offer these words as direct translations?

Tarski, to whom the three satisfaction conditions are due, saw their purpose the other way around; not as explaining negation, conjunction, and quantification, which would be untenable, but as contributing to a definition of satisfaction itself and so, derivatively, of truth. To begin with, let us go back down and define satisfaction for the simple sentences, or predications. Here we shall have a definition corresponding to each predicate of the object language, as follows.

The sentence consisting of 'walks', accompanied by the alphabetically *i*th variable, is satisfied by a sequence if and only if the *i*th thing in the sequence walks.

The sentence consisting of 'conquered', flanked by the alphabetically *i*th and *j*th variables, is satisfied by a sequence if and only if the *i*th thing in the sequence conquered the *j*th.

Similarly for each further predicate, supposing them finite in number and listed. In this way, one is told what it means to say of any predication in the object language that it is satisfied by a given sequence of things. One is told this only insofar, of course, as one already understands the predicates themselves; for note how 'walks' and 'conquered' got reused in the explanatory parts of the above two paragraphs.

Sentences may be graded in point of complexity. Predications have complexity 0; negations and existential quantifications of sentences of complexity n have complexity $n + 1$; and conjunctions have complexity $n + 1$ if one of the constituents has complexity n and the other has n or less. What one was last told, then, was what it means for a sequence to satisfy a sentence of complexity 0. But then the satisfaction conditions for negation, conjunction, and existential quantification tell one what it means for a sequence to satisfy a sentence of next higher complexity, once one knows what it means for a sequence to satisfy a sentence of given complexity. So, step by step, one finds out what it means for a sequence to satisfy a sentence of any preassigned complexity. Complexity n, for each n, takes n such steps.

This plan affords a definition of satisfaction, for all sentences of the object language, which is *recursive* or *inductive*. Starting with simple cases and building up, it sets forth, case by case, the circumstances in which to say that a sequence satisfies a sentence. Let us review this inductive definition schematically. Let us call the ith variable of the alphabet var(i). Let the ith thing in any sequence x be x_i. Then, if we think of 'A' as one of the one-place predicates of the object language, the inductive definition of satisfaction begins thus:

> (1) For all i and x: x satisfies 'A' followed by var(i) if and only if Ax_i.

There is such a clause for each one-place predicate in the lexicon. Similarly for each two-place predicate, 'B' say:

> (2) For all i, j, and x: x satisfies 'B' followed by var(i) and var(j) if and only if Bx_ix_j.

After making such a provision for each predicate in the lexicon, the recursive definition concludes as follows.

> (3) For all sequences x and sentences y: x satisfies the negation of y if and only if x does not satisfy y.

(4) For all sequences x and sentences y and y': x satisfies the conjunction of y and y' if and only if x satisfies y and x satisfies y'.

(5) For all x, y, and i: x satisfies the existential quantification of y with respect to var(i) if and only if y is satisfied by some sequence x' such that $x_j = x_j'$ for all $j \neq i$.

Taken altogether, the inductive definition tells us what it is for a sequence to satisfy a sentence of the object language. Incidentally it affords a definition also of truth, since, as lately noted, this just means being satisfied by all sequences.

Definitions come in two grades. At its best, definition enables us to eliminate and dispense with the defined expression. Some definitions accomplish this by specifying a substitute expression outright. An example is the definition of '5' as '4 + 1', or of the universal quantifier '$\forall x$' as '$\sim\exists x\sim$'. Some definitions accomplish it rather by showing how to paraphrase all contexts of the defined expression. An example is definition of the particle 'or' of alternation by systematically explaining all its immediate contexts, 'p or q' in form, as '$\sim(\sim p . \sim q)$'. This definition offers no direct substitute for the particle 'or' itself, but still it serves to eliminate that particle wherever it might appear. Definition of either sort is called *direct* definition, and constitutes the higher grade.

Definition in the lower grade, on the other hand, does not eliminate. Still it completely fixes the use of the defined expression. Our inductive definition of satisfaction is of this kind. *It settles just what sequences satisfy each sentence,* but it does not show how to eliminate 'x satisfies y' with variable x and y.

With help of some heavy equipment from set theory, we can raise the one grade of definition to the other. We can define 'satisfies' directly and eliminably, granted set-theoretic resources. The reasoning is as follows.

We may think of a *relation* as a set of ordered pairs. The satisfaction relation is the set of all pairs $\langle x, y \rangle$ such that x satisfies y. Now the inductive definition (1)–(5) does settle just what pairs $\langle x, y \rangle$ belong to the satisfaction relation; for, note the sentence lately italicized. If, bringing in a variable 'z', we modify (1)–(5) to the extent of writing 'bears the relation z to' instead of 'satisfies', then the stipulations (1)–(5) thus modified compel z to be the satisfaction relation. If we abbreviate (1)–(5), thus modified, as 'SRz', then 'SRz' says in effect 'z is the satisfaction relation'. But now we have a direct definition of 'x satisfies y' after all. We can write 'x bears z to y' as '⟨x, y⟩ ∈ z' and then put 'x satisfies y' thus:

(6)   ∃z (SRz . ⟨x, y⟩ ∈ z).

Paradox in the object language We have arrived at a direct definition, (6), of satisfaction. In formulating it we have not limited ourselves to the means available within the object language with which this relation of satisfaction has to do. Let us next consider the possibility of reconstructing this definition within the object language itself. If we reckon the predicate '∈' of set theory to the lexicon of the object language, then all of (6) except the heavy clause 'SRz' goes over into the object language without a hitch. Even the complex term '⟨x, y⟩' resolves out, through contextual definitions that I shall not pause over. In the end (6) expands into just '∈', variables, truth functions, quantification, *and* 'SRz'. The requisite steps are evident from various logic and set-theory texts.

What now of 'SRz'? Its needs are just the needs of (1)–(5), minus 'satisfies' (which gave way everywhere to '∈ z'). Scanning (1)–(5), we see that we shall need not only to use but to talk *about* various simple and complex expressions: predicates, variables, negations, conjunctions, quantifiers; also that we shall need to talk of sequences and numbers, and to specify variables numerically, and to specify positions in sequences numerically. Now the talk of sequences and of numbers can be got down to set theory—ultimately to '∈', variables, truth functions, and quantifiers again. Similarly for identity, used in (5). As for the talk of expressions, it can be got down to these same elements plus a modest lexicon of special predicates for spelling. One of these is a three-place predicate 'C' of concatenation: 'Cxyz' means that x, y, and z are strings of signs and that x consists of y followed by z. The others are one-place predicates each of which identifies a single sign; thus 'Ax' might mean that x is the accent, 'Lx' might mean that x is the left-hand parenthesis, and so on. Passing over a mass of detail that is available elsewhere [1] to the interested reader, I shall simply report that 'SRz' reduces to this modest lexicon of predicates—'∈', 'C', 'A', 'L', and the rest—together with variables, truth functions, and quantification.

As a point of curiosity, I might remark that by an artifice of Gödel's we can even reduce this lexicon of predicates to '∈' alone.

---

[1] For example, in my *Mathematical Logic*, last chapter. But note that the ideas in the present section and the preceding two are Tarski's except for detail.

The artifice consists in letting positive integers go proxy for signs and strings of signs. Thus suppose, to make it easy, that our alphabet of signs runs to nine or fewer. We can arbitrarily identify these with the numbers from 1 to 9, and then identify each string of signs with the number expressed by the corresponding string of digits. By this indirection we can accomplish all the work of the spelling predicates 'C', 'A', 'L', etc., in arithmetical terms; and the arithmetic boils down in turn to 'ϵ', variables, truth functions, and quantification.

With or without this last refinement, we can see 'SRz' into the object language with its standard grammar and a specifiable lexicon of predicates. And so, through (6), 'x satisfies y' gets translated into the object language.

This news sounds cheerful, but we shall soon find cause to fret over it. Consider Grelling's paradox, commonly known as the heterological paradox. It can be phrased as having to do with open sentences in a single variable. All sorts of things can satisfy these sentences. Sentences satisfy some of them. Some of them satisfy themselves. The open sentence 'x is short' is a short sentence and thus satisfies itself. The open sentence 'x satisfies some sentences' satisfies some sentences and thus satisfies itself. Also many open sentences fail to satisfy themselves. Examples: 'x is long'; 'x is German'; 'nothing satisfies x'. Now try the open sentence 'x does not satisfy itself'. Clearly if it satisfies itself it does not, and vice versa.

This shows that 'x does not satisfy itself' must not get into the object language. For the object language already had, in its spelling predicates, the machinery by which to specify any of its own strings of signs as objects for its variables to refer to. If one of these strings of signs were 'x does not satisfy itself', or rather the full expansion thereof into the basic notation, then, by taking that very string of signs as the object to be referred to by 'x', we would get the contradiction.

But we just previously concluded that 'x satisfies y' is translatable into the object language, as a straightforward open sentence. But then '$\sim(x$ satisfies $x)$', or 'x does not satisfy itself', is translatable equally. Apparently then we are caught in contradiction.

Resolution in set theory Its resolution lies in set theory. The inductive definition represented by (1)–(5) was all right, and can be translated wholly into the object language except of course for the new term that is being inductively defined—the verb 'satisfies'. Accordingly 'SRz', which we get from (1)–(5) by dropping that verb and supplying '*z*', is fully translatable into the object language. Moreover, 'SR*z*' does indeed require of *z* that its member pairs be precisely the pairs $\langle x, y \rangle$ such that *x* satisfies *y*. So far so good. But *is there* a set *z* meeting this requirement? If so, (6) serves its purpose of defining '*x* satisfies *y*'; if not, (6) is simply false for all *x* and *y*. And the answer is indeed negative, by *reductio ad absurdum*; there is no such set *z*, or we would be back in Grelling's contradiction.

The general question what sets there are has been long and notoriously unsettled. An open sentence is said to determine a set if the sentence is true of all and only the members of the set. It is common sense to consider that we have specified the set when we have given the sentence; hence that every open sentence determines a set. But the paradoxes of set theory, notably Russell's, teach us otherwise; the sentence '$\sim(x \,\epsilon\, x)$' determines no set. If there were such a set, it would have to be a member of itself if and only if not a member of itself.

So the set theorist has to try to settle which open sentences still to regard as determining sets. Different choices give different set theories, some stronger than others. When we accorded 'ϵ' to the lexicon of our object language, we left open the question how strong a set theory was to go with it. But of this we can now be sure: it cannot, consistently with the the rest of the object language, be a set theory containing a set *z* such that SR*z*.

Tarski's work thus forges a new link between the so-called semantical paradoxes, of which Grelling's is the prime example, and the set-theoretic paradoxes, of which Russell's is the prime example. At any rate we have been forced by Grelling's paradox to repudiate a supposed set *z*. But it should be noted that this repudiation is a weaker paradox than Russell's in this respect: the *z* that it repudiates was not a set that was purportedly determined by any open sentence expressible in the object language. It purported indeed to be the set of all pairs $\langle x, y \rangle$ such that *x* satisfies *y*, and so it purported indeed to be determined by the open sentence '*x* satisfies *y*'. But this is not a sentence of the object language. As Grelling's paradox has taught us, it is untranslatable foreign language.

We can still accept '*x* satisfies *y*' as a sentence of the metalanguage, and at that level we can even accept it as determining a set *z*. On these terms, (6) is acceptable still as defining '*x* satisfies *y*'; but as defining it in the metalanguage for the object language. The metalanguage can tolerate a stronger set theory than the object language can; it can tolerate a set *z* such that SR*z*.

It should be mentioned that the resistance of a language to its satisfaction predicate is not absolute. A language can contain its own satisfaction predicate and truth predicate with impunity if, unlike what we have considered, it is weak in auxiliary devices that would be needed in reaping the contradictions.[1]

[1] There is an example in John R. Myhill, "A complete theory of natural, rational, and real numbers," *Journal of Symbolic Logic*, 15 (1950), 185–96.

LOGICAL TRUTH

4

In terms
of structure
Our study of the notion of truth turned into a study of the notion of satisfaction. Truth is the limiting case of satisfaction, as the closed sentence is the limiting case of the sentence. In order to formulate the notion of truth of closed sentences we had to ascend inductively by way of the satisfaction of open sentences. The reason is that even closed sentences are composed of open constituent sentences. This was the insight that led Tarski to his celebrated definition of truth, and of satisfaction, which we have been studying.

The satisfaction conditions for negation, conjunction, and existential quantification played a central role in the inductive definition of satisfaction. But these conditions are also worth noting apart from defining anything, simply as affording the basis of a logical calculus of negation, conjunction, and existential quantification. These conditions determine, for each compound sentence, just what sequences satisfy it, given the same information regarding the atomic sentences.

This determinacy does not sort itself out over the several sequences. That is, you could know what atomic sentences a sequence satisfies and yet have no way of deciding whether it satisfies a certain compound sentence. You could know what atomic sentences a sequence $\langle a, b \rangle$ satisfies and have no way of deciding whether it satisfies a quantification '$\exists z\ Fxyz$'. For this is the question whether $\langle a, b, w \rangle$ satisfies '$Fxyz$' for at least one thing w; and this question outruns all the atomic information about $\langle a, b \rangle$. Higher-level information about $\langle a, b \rangle$ depends on simple information about more than $\langle a, b \rangle$ itself. But all the higher-level information is nevertheless determinate relative to the infinite totality, however unmanageable, of simple information. Given what sequences satisfy the simple sentences, altogether, it is settled what sequences satisfy any compound sentence.

These determining links are the business of logic. It is not for logic to settle what sequences satisfy the simple sentences, but rather, contingently on such information, to settle what compound sentences will be true or what sequences will satisfy them. Equally logic explores these connections in reverse: given that a compound sentence is true, or given what satisfies it, to settle what alternatives are left open for the simple sentences. Indirectly also, through these dependences upward and downward, there are transverse interdependences to explore between one compound sentence and another.

A familiar connection of the kind is *logical implication*. One closed sentence logically implies another when, on the assumption that the one is true, the structures of the two sentences assure that the other is true. The crucial restriction here is that no supporting supplementary assumption or information be invoked as to the truth of additional sentences. Logical implication rests wholly on how the truth functions, quantifiers, and variables stack up. It rests wholly on what we may call, in a word, the logical structure of the two sentences.

Logical implication applies likewise to open sentences. One open sentence logically implies another if only those sequences satisfy the one that satisfy the other—provided, again, that this is assured by the logical structure of the two sentences themselves, unsupplemented by other information.

Logical implication is one of a family of closely related notions. Another is *logical incompatibility*. Closed sentences are logically incompatible when their joint truth is precluded by their logical structure. Open sentences are logically incompatible when their logical structure precludes their joint satisfaction by any sequence.

Other members of the family are *logical truth* and *logical falsity*. A logically true (or false) sentence is a sentence whose truth (or falsity) is assured by its logical structure.

A convention adopted early in Chapter 3, by the way, is saving us phrases; namely, the convention of calling open sentences true that are true for all values of their free variables. In the present chapter these savings are appreciable.

We may conveniently subordinate this family of notions to one of their number, the notion of logical truth. Its advantage over implication is that it takes sentences singly rather than in pairs. The other notions can be got out of logical truth as follows. A sentence is logically false just in case its negation is logically true. Two or more sentences are logically incompatible just in case their conjunction is logically false. And one sentence logically implies another, finally, when logically incompatible with the other's negation. Or, not to stop there, we may add equivalence: sentences are *logically equivalent* that imply each other.

In all this last lot of formulations I have been able to dispense with the distinction between open and closed sentences, thanks to the convention.

I defined a logical truth as a sentence whose truth is assured by its logical structure. To avoid a possible misunderstanding, however, it is better to put the matter more explicitly thus: a sentence is logically true if all sentences are true that share its logical structure. But at this point a subtle distinction must be noted: it can happen that one sentence has the entire logical structure of another and yet not *vice versa*. For instance the sentence:

$$(1) \qquad \sim\exists x \, (x \text{ floats} \, . \, \sim(x \text{ floats}) \,)$$

has all the logical structure of:

$$(2) \qquad \sim\exists x \, (x \text{ floats} \, . \, x \text{ burns}).$$

It also has a bit more; enough more to be, unlike (2), logically true. All sentences that have the entire logical structure of (1) are true; and therein lies the logical truth of (1). Not all sentences that have the logical structure of (2) are true; (1) is, but (2) itself is not.

In terms of substitution I have explained that what I mean by the logical structure of a sentence, at this stage, is its composition in respect of truth functions, quantifiers, and variables. It follows that logical structure and predicates are all there is to a sentence, under the standard grammar we have adopted. Just put schematic letters 'F', 'G', etc., in place of the predicates in a sentence, and you have depicted its logical structure.

This suggests another and simpler way of defining logical truth: a sentence is logically true if it stays true under all changes of its predicates. But at this point another distinction must be noted, subtler than the one previously brought out by (1) and (2). It turns on how liberally we read "changes of its predicates." On an illiberal reading, this would mean merely substitution of predicates for predicates. A change of predicate in this sense turns the sentence:

(3) $\quad\quad\quad\quad\quad\quad$ $\exists x\ (x$ floats . x burns)

into:

(4) $\quad\quad\quad\quad\quad\quad$ $\exists x\ (x$ floats . x dissolves)

but not into:

(5) $\quad\quad\quad\quad\quad\quad$ $\exists x\ (x$ floats . $\sim(x$ floats)).

In defining logical truth we want of course the more liberal reading; we want to count (5) as sharing the logical structure of (3). What is in point is not substitution of predicates for predicates, but substitution of sentences ('$\sim(x$ floats)', 'x dissolves') for simple sentences ('x burns').

A *logical truth*, then, is definable *as a sentence from which we get only truths when we substitute sentences for its simple sentences*. Thus (3) is not logically true, since substitution of the complex sentence '$\sim(x$ floats)' for the simple sentence 'x burns' in (3) yields a falsehood, (5). On the other hand (1) is logically true, because whenever a sentence, however complex, is substituted for 'x floats' in (1) the result is still true.

Sometimes this definition of logical truth is given in two stages, mediated by the notion of a *valid logical schema*. A logical schema is a dummy sentence of the sort touched upon a page back. It is like a sentence except that it has schematic letters 'F', 'G', etc., in place of predicates. In other words, it is built up by quantifiers and truth functions from simple sentence schemata such as 'Fxy', 'Fzx', 'Gz', etc. (One could allow also the schematic letters 'p', 'q', etc.; but it will be simpler at this stage to skip them.) A logical schema is *valid* if every sentence obtainable from it by substituting sentences for simple sentence schemata is true. A *logical truth*, finally, is a truth thus obtainable from a valid logical schema. This two-step definition of logical truth amounts to the same thing as the one-step one italicized in the preceding paragraph. The reason for the two-step version is just that the notion of a valid schema is of further utility. Because of their freedom from subject matter, schemata are the natural medium for logical laws and proofs.

The one-step definition speaks of substituting sentences for simple sentences; the two-step one speaks of substituting sentences for simple schemata. In either case the substitutions must of course be uniform. If the sentence:

$$\sim(x \text{ floats } . \ x \text{ is denser than } y)$$

is what we are substituting for the simple sentence '$x > y$' (or for the simple schema 'Fxy'), then we must also substitute:

$$\sim(z \text{ floats } . \ z \text{ is denser than } x)$$

for '$z > x$' (or 'Fzx'). Full formulation of this requirement is rather fussy, and I shall not pause over it. It is covered in logic texts.[1]

In terms of models
But I shall have much more to say of validity. The definition of validity now before us refers to substitution; a schema is valid if substitution in it yields none but true sentences. A very different definition of validity is also worth knowing: one that makes use of set theory. We may best understand it with help of two preliminary notions. One is the notion of the *set-theoretic analogue*, as I shall call it, of a logical schema. This is a certain open sentence of set theory that we form from the schema in the following way. We change the predications 'Fx', 'Fy', 'Gx', etc., to read '$x \in \alpha$', '$y \in \alpha$', '$x \in \beta$', etc., thus invoking variables 'α', 'β', etc., whose values are to be sets. We handle two-place predicate letters with help of ordered pairs, thus changing 'Hxy' to read '$\langle x, y \rangle \in \gamma$'. Correspondingly for three-place predicate letters and higher. The logical schema '$\exists x (Fx . Gx)$', for instance, has the open sentence '$\exists x (x \in \alpha . x \in \beta)$' as its set-theoretic analogue. This sentence talks of sets and invites quantifiers '$\forall \alpha$', '$\exists \beta$', '$\forall \beta$', whereas the schematic letters 'F' and 'G' merely simulate predicates and are not value-taking variables at all. The schema is a dummy, depicting the logical form of certain sentences; its set-theoretic analogue, on the other hand, is one of the

---

[1] Quine, *Methods of Logic*, 4th ed. (Cambridge: Harvard, 1982), § 26-28, and *Elementary Logic*, rev. ed. (Cambridge: Harvard, 1966), §§ 40-42.

actual sentences of that logical form. It is an open sentence, satisfied by some sequences of sets and not by others.

A second notion that will figure in the new definition of validity is that of a *model*. A model of a schema is a sequence of sets: one set corresponding to each schematic predicate letter in the schema, and, as the initial set of the sequence, a non-empty set U to play the role of universe or range of values of the variables 'x', 'y', etc. The set in the model corresponding to a one-place predicate letter of the schema is a set of members of U; the set corresponding to a two-place predicate letter is a set of pairs of members of U; and so on. A model is said to satisfy a schema if, briefly, it satisfies the set-theoretic analogue of the schema. More fully: the model satisfies the schema if, when we specify U as the range of values of the variables 'x', 'y', etc., and we assign the further sets of the model to the respective set variables 'α', 'β', etc., the set-theoretic analogue of the schema comes out true.

A model (U, α, β) satisfies the logical schema '$\exists x\, (Fx \,.\, Gx)$', for instance, if $\exists x\, (x \in \alpha \,.\, x \in \beta)$; hence if the two sets in the model overlap. The model satisfies the schema '$\sim\exists x\, (Fx \,.\, \sim Gx)$' if the one set is a subset of the other.

Now the new definition of validity is this: a schema is valid if satisfied by all its models. A logical truth, finally, is as before: any sentence obtainable by substitution in a valid schema.

The conspicuous difference between the new definition of validity and the old is that the new one talks of all assignments of sets where the old talked of all substitutions of sentences. Our next business will be to assess this difference.

An incidental difference is the variability of U; the old definition supposed a fully interpreted object language with no option left open as to range of variables. As for the stipulation that U not be empty, it is strictly a technical convenience and no philosophical dogma about necessary existence. Its convenience arises from a peculiarity of the number 0. There is an easy proof that if a schema is satisfied by all models in bigger universes it is satisfied by all models in smaller universes too, except only, sometimes, the empty universe; hence we set the empty universe aside so as not to immobilize a lot of otherwise valid and valuable schemata. There is no enigma about the empty universe; its logic can be managed separately, and is indeed a triumph of triviality.[1]

---

[1] See, e.g., *Methods of Logic*, p. 117.

Let us now ponder the main contrast: that between assignment of sets and substitution of sentences. If every open sentence determined a set and every set were determined by a sentence, then the contrast would dissolve; assignment of sets to the predicate letters and substitution of sentences for the simple schemata would come to the same thing. But in fact there are set shortages and there are sentence shortages; neither does every open sentence determine a set nor is every set determined by a sentence.

These reciprocal shortages are neatly illustrated by the two paradoxes, Russell's and Grelling's. In view of Russell's paradox we know an open sentence of the object language, namely, '$\sim(x \in x)$', that determines no set. In view of Grelling's paradox we know a set which is determined by no sentence of the object language; namely, the set of all sentences of the object language that do not satisfy themselves. If a sentence determined this set, the sentence would be '$\sim(x$ satisfies $x)$' or an equivalent; and Grelling's paradox shows that no such sentence is admissible in the object language.

Adequacy of substitution These twin discrepancies between sets and sentences could lead us to expect a discrepancy between the two definitions of validity. However, two remarkable theorems assure us, on the contrary, that neither the set shortage nor the sentence shortage will have any bearing on the definition of validity as long as our object language is reasonably rich: rich enough for elementary number theory. Any schema that comes out true under all substitutions of sentences, in such a language, will also be satisfied by all models; and conversely.

The demand that the object language be rich enough for elementary number theory is a moderate demand. Elementary number theory comprises only what can be said about positive integers in terms of plus, times, identity, truth functions, and quantification; no sets. For purposes of our standard grammar the plus and times functors would of course be absorbed into appropriate predicates along with identity (see Chapter 2).

Precisely the schemata that are true under all substitutions of sentences, in such a language, are satisfied by all models; such is the remarkable fact that can be proved. More explicitly, what we get are these two theorems:

(I)   If a schema comes out true under all substitutions of sentences of elementary number theory, it is satisfied by every model.

(II) If a schema is satisfied by every model, it comes out true under all substitutions of sentences.

The roots of (I) are in 1915. That was when Leopold Löwenheim argued that *every schema satisfied by a model at all is satisfied by some model* ⟨U, α, β, γ, . . .⟩ *where U is limited to the positive integers*. Hilbert and Bernays subsequently strengthened this result by stipulating that each of the sets α, β, γ, . . . be determined by a sentence of elementary number theory.[1] Thus

(A) If a schema is satisfied by a model at all, it becomes true under some substitution of sentences of elementary number theory for its simple schemata.

We have to suppose, of course, that when these substitutions are made the variables of quantification are construed as counting the positive integers among their values. But it is all right for them to take other things as values besides; this is easily shown.[2]

We can argue from (A) to (I) as follows. (A) is equivalent, by contraposition, to saying that if a schema is false under all substitutions of sentences of elementary number theory then it is satisfied by no model. But if instead of talking about a schema we talk about its negation, then 'false' in this phrasing changes to 'true' and 'satisfied by no model' changes to 'satisfied by all models'; and so we have (I).[3]

The background of (II) is the theorem of the deductive completeness of the logic of quantification. It goes back to Skolem, Herbrand, and Gödel (1928–1930), and runs thus:[4]

(B) If a schema is satisfied by every model, it can be proved.

The word 'proved' here may be taken as alluding to some method of proof appearing in logic textbooks; the completeness theorem (B) can be established for each of various such methods. Some of those methods, moreover, are visibly sound: visibly such as to generate only schemata that come out true under all substitutions. Taking the proof method alluded to in (B) as such a method, we infer (II).

In (I) and (II) I see good reason for resting with the definition of validity that we had got to first; namely, truth under substitutions

---

[1] Op. cit., § 33.   [2] Op. cit., p. 117.
[3] David Makinson has noted that we must complicate this argument a bit if the schema contains free '*x*', '*y*', etc.
[4] Op. cit., § 32.

of sentences for the simple component schemata. This means resting with the definition of logical truth that we got to at that point. Stated without the detour through valid schemata, it is this: a sentence is *logically true* if *only truths come of it by substitution of sentences for its simple component sentences.* The theorems (I) and (II) assure us that this definition of logical truth agrees with the alternative definition in terms of models, as long as the object language is not too weak for the modest idioms of elementary number theory. In the contrary case we can as well blame any discrepancies on the weakness of the language as on the definition of logical truth.

Saving on sets   The evident philosophical advantage of resting with this substitutional definition, and not broaching model theory, is that we save on ontology. Sentences suffice, sentences even of the object language, instead of a universe of sets specifiable and unspecifiable.

In enterprises other than definition of logical truth there continues, indeed, to be reason for acquiescing in some of the ontological excesses of set theory. It is in set theory that a general systematic foundation is contrived for mathematics. Parts of mathematics, however, require less lavish resources in set theory than other parts, and it is a good plan to keep track of the differences. In this way, when occasions arise for revising theories, we are in a position to favor theories whose demands are lighter. So we have progressed a step whenever we find a way of cutting the ontological costs of some particular development. This is true equally outside of mathematics, and it is true in particular of the definition of logical truth.

Theorems (A) and (B) and their corollaries (I) and (II) remain remarkable theorems of model theory, unaided by the word 'valid' or the phrase 'logically true'. (I) and (II) are, more particularly, theorems of model theory that assure us that we do not need to broach model theory to talk adequately of validity and logical truth. (I) and (II) assure us that we can define validity and logical truth adequately by talking merely of sentence substitution.

It would be inaccurate, still, to say that by retreating to the substitutional definitions of validity and logical truth we have rendered the notions of validity and logical truth wholly independent of sets. In talking of sentences and substitution at all we might be held still to be talking of sets; for, what is a sentence but the set of its tokens?

The case is yet worse; sets of tokens will not suffice. A sentence that happens to be destined never to get written or uttered would be, as a set of tokens, the empty set. Any two such sentences would count as identical. Sentences would thus simply not exist, in any useful sense, except insofar as eventually written or uttered. On the other hand anyone familiar with how the theorem (A) is proved will know that there can be no such limitation on the sentences whose substitution is talked of in (A). (A) would cease to be true on such terms, and so would (I), and thus the very justification of our retreat to the substitutional definitions of validity and logical truth would go by the board. (A) depends rather upon a classical, infinite theory of finite strings of signs. Whenever x and y are different strings, x followed by z must count as a different string from y followed by z even if never written or uttered.

A way of meeting this demand is by taking a string of signs not as a set of tokens but as a sequence, in the mathematical sense, of its signs; a sequence in the sense of Chapter 3. The component individual signs or phonemes of the string can still be taken as the sets of *their* tokens, since we can see to the existence of such tokens. Thus construed, strings of signs are assured in the unlimited supply required by (A). But in invoking finite sequences thus without limit of length we have drawn further on set theory.

Alternatively we may identify signs and strings of signs outright with positive integers, followed Gödel (see Chapter 3). Elementary number theory is in effect equivalent still to a certain amount of set theory, as is the theory of finite sequences, but either way it is a modest part: the theory of finite sets. And anyway we were committed to admitting elementary number theory even into our object language when we accepted (I) as justifying our retreat to the substitutional definitions of validity and logical truth. The way to look upon that retreat, then, is this: it renders the notions of validity and logical truth independent of all but a modest bit of set theory; independent of the higher flights.

In terms of proof But we must not lose sight of another very substantial notion that figures still in these substitutional definitions; namely, the notion of truth. These definitions explain validity and logical truth as truth under all substitutions. This general notion of a true sentence, like the notion of satisfaction, is so considerable a notion that it exceeds even the bounds of the object language.

This dependence upon the notion of truth is not a price paid for the retreat to the substitutional definitions of validity and logical truth. The definitions in terms of models appealed equally to truth, or satisfaction. Therefore this dependence is no reason to reconsider our choice between these two pairs of definitions. It is, however, a reason to examine a third pair which is independent of the notions of truth and satisfaction.

The key to these new definitions is the completeness theorem, (B) above. We can simply describe the moves that constitute one of those complete proof procedures, and then define a valid schema as a schema that can be proved by such moves. Then we can define a logical truth derivatively as before: as a sentence obtainable by substituting for the simple schemata in a valid schema. Actually some of those complete methods of proof do not require schemata, but can be applied outright rather to the sentences that would be the results of substitution in the schemata.[1] Such a method serves to generate logically true sentences directly from other logically true sentences. If we choose one of these proof procedures, we can skip schemata and validity; we can simply define a logical truth as any sentence produced by these rules of proof.

Any such proposal, to define validity or logical truth in terms of a proof procedure, tends to call forth a clamor of protest. It is protested that the property of being provable by the chosen proof procedure is intrinsically uninteresting; it derives its interest solely from the completeness theorem, which equates it to logical truth in a prior and intrinsically interesting sense. It is protested also that in so defining logical truth we would pull the rug from under the important completeness theorem itself, depriving it of content.

Actually no such matters are at stake. The completeness theorem as formulated in (B) is independent of how we define logical truth, since it does not mention logical truth by name. Part of its importance is that it shows that we *can* define logical truth by mere description of a proof procedure, without loss of any of the traits that may have made logical truth interesting to us in the first place.

The theorems establishing equivalence among very unlike formulations of a notion—logical truth or whatever—are of course the important part. Which of the formulations we choose as the somehow official definition is less important. But even in such verbal matters there are better and worse choices. The more elementary of two definitions has the advantage of relevance to a wider range of collateral studies.

It should be said, however, that part of the resistance to this elementary way of defining logical truth has a special reason: the arbitrariness of choice among proof procedures. One feels he has missed the essence of logical truth when his definition is arbitrary to that degree.

[1] One such is the "main method," op cit., § 30.

Just how elementary is this manner of definition? It describes rules of proofs and thus talks of strings of signs. On this score it is on a par with the definition that appeals to substitution of sentences; it operates, in effect, at the level of elementary number theory. But it keeps to that level, whereas the other definition invoked also the notion of truth. This is the great difference.

In terms of grammar We have seen several ways of defining logical truth. They are extensionally equivalent: they all declare the same sentences logically true (supposing the object language reasonably rich in predicates). They differ markedly in their apparatus, but they all hinge upon sameness of structure in respect of three grammatical constructions that are local to the object language: negation, conjunction, quantification. A definition of logical truth may be so phrased as to mention these constructions explicitly, or it may allude to them indirectly by talking of substitution for simple sentences or simple schemata; the difference is of no moment, the two idioms being correlative and complementary.

Now the further idea suggests itself of defining logical truth more abstractly, by appealing not specifically to the negation, conjunction, and quantification that figure in our particular object language, but to whatever grammatical constructions one's object language may contain. A logical truth is, on this approach, a sentence whose grammatical structure is such that all sentences with that structure are true.

Sentences have the same grammatical structure when they are interconvertible by lexical substitutions. Our new definition of logical truth, then, can also be put thus: a *logical truth is a truth that cannot be turned false by substituting for lexicon.* When for its lexical elements we substitute any other strings belonging to the same grammatical categories, the resulting sentence is true.

The lexicon of our own object language consists of just the predicates and the three unaccented variables: 'x', 'y', 'z'. Applied here, therefore, the effect of the above suggestion would be to count a sentence as logically true so long as it stays true under all substitutions of predicates for predicates and variables for unaccented variables.

The odd exclusion of substitution for accented variables does not prevent substituting 'y''''' for 'x'''' in effect, for we can get the effect by substituting 'y''' for the initial 'x' of 'x''''. We are concerned here not with substitution of some sophisticatedly logical sort, but with flatly grammatical substitution within our stated constructions; and accentuation is one of the constructions. Thus the lexical quirk in the variables has only this effect on the definition of logical truth: it takes no account of substitutions that diminish the number of accents. Surely this is of no moment. For surely, if a sentence could be turned false by some relettering that did diminish accents, it can still be turned false by another relettering that does not.

But variables raise also another problem, as Harman has pointed out:[1] grammatical structure properly so called is not always preserved when we put some variable for all occurrences of an old one, and neither is logical truth. This difficulty might be met by requiring that substitution be understood as *conservative*; that is, the substituted variable or other lexical element must be new to the context. This needlessly restricts substitution for predicates, but not, I think, in such a way as to change the demarcation of the logical truths. An interesting alternative suggestion of Harman's is that we reclassify variables as particles rather than lexicon, by changing the criteria of lexicon on page 29. "Instead of counting both infiniteness of category and indefiniteness of category as criteria, one could make do with indefiniteness."

Our definition of logical truth in terms of substitution of lexicon confronts also another and graver difficulty: it appeals only to substitution of predicates for predicates, as against substitution of sentences for simple sentences. We saw early in this chapter how the sentential approach could issue in a stronger, narrower concept of logical truth, screening out some cases that would have slipped through if only predicate substitution had been called for. It can even be shown that the version in terms of predicate substitution will inevitably be too weak, as long as our stock of predicates is finite.[2] The natural remedy, then, is to exploit the indefiniteness of our category of predicates: to admit substitution not only of the predicates in some imagined list, but also of any predicates that might be added. Thus adjusted, then, the abstract version runs as follows: *a logical truth is a sentence that cannot be turned false by substituting for lexicon, even under supplementation of lexical resources.*

So far as our object language is concerned, we do quite well to rest with one or another of the definitions of logical truth already reached in earlier pages. Where the new and more abstract sugges-

---

[1] Gilbert Harman, review in *Metaphilosophy*, 1971.
[2] This was pointed out to me by Mark L. Wilson.

tion has its value is in the consideration of other languages. In this connection we do well to note, as we just now did, that the earlier definitions agree with this more abstract one as long as the lexicon of predicates is not too cramped.

The definition is still not transcendent. It hinges on the notion of a grammatical construction, or, in the complementary phrasing, the notion of lexicon. We have no defensible transcendent notion of construction or lexicon, but only a loosely related family of mutually more or less analogous immanent notions (see Chapter 2). One and the same language, indeed—one and the same infinite set of sentences, anyway—can of course be generated by different constructions from different lexical beginnings. Our proposed abstract notion of logical truth depends not only on the language but on how we grammaticize it.

The suggestion does nevertheless offer a welcome gain in generality, and, in addition, a notable connection between logic and grammar. What sentences of a language to count as logically true is determined, on this theory, when we have settled two things about the language: its grammar and its truth predicate. Logic is, in the jargon of mechanics, the resultant of two components: grammar and truth.

THE SCOPE OF LOGIC

5

Various definitions of logical truth that we have surveyed involve varying the simple constituents of a compound sentence,
or schematizing and reapplying the outward structure of a compound sentence. They are all predicated on grammatical structure.

This whole attitude toward logical truth is threatened, however,
by the predicate '=' of identity. Truths of identity theory such as
'$x = x$', or again '$\exists y\ (x = y)$' or '$\sim(x = y.\ \sim(y = x)\ )$', do not
qualify as logical truths under the contemplated definitions of logical
truth, since they are falsifiable by substituting other predicates
for '='.

Should we accept the conclusion that the truth '$x = x$' and its
kin are not logical truths, and accordingly look upon identity as
extra-logical? Should we view the predicate '=', along with '>' and
'ϵ', as proper not to logic but to extra-logical mathematics? In one
way this conclusion seems fitting. We remarked, toward the end of
Chapter 1, on the typical obliquity of logical generalities; it was
what drove us to semantic ascent. If on the other hand we were to
count '=' or any other predicate as purely logical vocabulary, then
we would have to recognize some logical generalities as expressible
by direct quantification in the object language after all; for instance,
'$\forall x\ (x = x)$'. This seems unfortunate. The contrast between generalities that can be expressed thus by a quantification in the object
language, on the one hand, and generalities on the other hand that
call for semantic ascent, marks a conspicuous and tempting place at
which to draw the line between the other sciences and logic.

But there are also reasons for preferring, on the contrary, to reckon identity theory to logic. One respect in which identity theory seems a nearer neighbor to logic than to mathematics is its completeness. Complete proof procedures are available not only for quantification theory (cf. (B) of Chapter 4) but for quantification theory and identity theory together. Gödel has shown that the axiom:

$$(1) \qquad\qquad x = x$$

and the axiom schema:

$$(2) \qquad\qquad {\sim}(x = y \,.\, Fx \,.\, {\sim}Fy),$$

when added to a complete proof procedure for quantification theory, afford a complete proof procedure for quantification and identity.[1] Elementary number theory, in contrast, is shown in Gödel's more famous theorem (1931) to admit no complete proof procedure.[2]

Another respect in which identity theory seems more like logic than mathematics is universality: it treats of all objects impartially. Any theory can indeed likewise be formulated with general variables, ranging over everything, but still the only values of the variables that matter to number theory, for instance, or set theory, are the numbers and the sets; whereas identity theory knows no preferences.

This latter trait suggests that identity theory, like quantification theory, is peculiarly basic. This is suggested also by the following fact: as soon as we have merely specified the truth-functional notations, the variables, and the open sentences of a language, we have already' settled enough to know what to count as an adequate definition of identity for that language. An open sentence whose free variables are 'x' and 'y' will serve the purpose of '$x = y$' if and only if it fulfills (1) and (2) for all objects x and y and all substitutions for 'Fx' and 'Fy'. It is easy to see that these conditions permit no latitude; any two definitions of identity that meet these conditions will coincide in all their attributions of identity. For, let us picture two such versions of identity as '$x =_1 y$' and '$x =_2 y$'. By (2), then, '${\sim}(x =_1 y \,.\, Fx \,.\, {\sim}Fy)$' holds under all substitutions for 'Fx' and 'Fy'. So

$$ {\sim}(x =_1 y \,.\, x =_2 x \,.\, {\sim}(x =_2 y)). $$

---

[1] See Jean van Heijenoort, ed., *From Frege to Gödel* (Cambridge: Harvard, 1967), p. 589 (Theorem VII).
[2] See *Methods of Logic*, § 34.

But, by (1), $x =_2 x$. So $\sim(x =_1 y . \sim(x =_2 y))$. Similarly $\sim(x =_2 y . \sim(x =_1 y))$. In short, $x =_1 y . \equiv . x =_2 y$.

Identity
reduced
The affinity of identity theory to logic is seen also in the following remarkable circumstance. An identity predicate is virtually at hand, without separate assumption, in any language whose grammar is of the kind we have called standard. Although we cannot define identity in terms purely of truth functions and quantification, we can define it or a serviceable facsimile in the systems where truth functions and quantifiers are applied.

The method of definition is evident from the following example. Consider a standard language whose lexicon of predicates consists of a one-place predicate 'A', two two-place predicates 'B' and 'C' and a three-place predicate 'D'. We then define '$x = y$' as short for:

(3) $Ax \equiv Ay . \forall z (Bzx \equiv Bzy . Bxz \equiv Byz . Czx \equiv Czy .$
   $Cxz \equiv Cyz . \forall z' (Dzz'x \equiv Dzz'y . Dzxz' \equiv Dzyz' .$
   $Dxzz' \equiv Dyzz'))$.

Note the plan: the exhaustion of combinations. What '$x = y$' tells us, according to this definition, is that the objects x and y are indistinguishable by the four predicates; that they are indistinguishable from each other even in their relations to any other objects z and z', insofar as these relations are expressed in simple sentences. Now it can be shown that, when (3) holds, the objects x and y will be indistinguishable by any sentences whatever, simple or not, that can be phrased in the language.

It may happen that the objects intended as values of the variables of quantification are not completely distinguishable from one another by the four predicates. When this happens, (3) fails to define genuine identity. Still, such failure remains unobservable from within the language; (3) is as good as identity from that vantage point. It is readily seen that the axiom (1), '$x = x$', is a truth purely of the logic of quantification and truth functions when '$=$' is defined by (3). It can be shown further that (2) becomes a valid schema of quantification theory.[1]

This method of defining or simulating identity depends on finitude of the lexicon of predicates, since the analogue of (3) for an infinitude of predicates would never end. Even where there are

---

[1] The proof follows the lines of *Mathematical Logic*, § 18.

infinitely many predicates we can commonly define identity, but not always.[1] Anyway the case of infinitely many predicates is, of course, a departure from our standard grammar; it requires some further grammatical construction for generating complex predicates, since a lexicon can only be finite.

The upshot is, I feel, that identity theory has stronger affinities with its neighbors in logic than with its neighbors in mathematics. It belongs in logic. Yet we saw it as a threat to our structurally conceived definitions of logical truth. Where does this leave us?

A reconciliation is afforded, curiously enough, by the very consideration that counted most strongly for reckoning identity theory to logic; namely, the definability of identity illustrated in (3). If, instead of reckoning ' $=$ ' to the lexicon of our object language as a simple predicate, we understand all equations as mere abbreviations of complex sentences along the lines of (3), then all laws of identity become mere abbreviations of logical truths of the purely quantificational sort: logical truths in the sense or senses of the preceding chapter. The structural view of logical truth is sustained.

When identity theory is studied, as it normally is, in abstraction from any specific object language and specific lexicon of predicates, it may be seen as schematic. Already in the logic of truth functions and quantifiers the schematic style prevails; we use schematic predicate letters to represent the unspecified predicates of an unspecified language and the compound open sentences constructible from them. In the same spirit the notation ' $x = y$ ' itself can be viewed schematically as representing the compound sentence to which those unspecified predicates would give rise by the construction typified in (3).

Set theory   We turn now from identity theory to set theory. Does it belong to logic? I shall conclude not.

The predicate ' ϵ ' of membership is distinctive of set theory, as is ' $=$ ' of the logic of identity. The language of pure set theory, taken in isolation from other subject matter, may be seen as a standard language in the sense of the middle of Chapter 2 but with ' ϵ ' as the only predicate in its lexicon. Thus its lexicon comprises just ' ϵ ', ' x ', ' y ', and ' z ', and its constructions are predication, negation, conjunction, existential quantification, and the accentuation of variables.

Alternatively, as was suggested later in Chapter 2, we may de-

[1] See my *Set Theory and Its Logic* (Cambridge: Harvard, 1963, 1969), p. 15.

mote the unique predicate to the status of a particle. This means listing the lexicon as just 'x', 'y', and 'z', and the constructions now as negation, conjunction, existential quantification, accentuation, and, instead of predication, a membership construction. This construction applies to two variables and yields a sentence, by interposing the particle 'ϵ'. The set-theoretic language remains the same whether we state its grammar in the first way or in the second. I shall favor the first, for its conformity to our more general talk of standard languages.

Besides 'ϵ', another conspicuous notation in set theory is the notation '$\{x: Fx\}$' or '$\hat{x}Fx$' of abstraction, which names a set in terms of an open sentence that determines it. However, this is eliminable by paraphrasing the sentences that contain it. One of these containing sentences is, for example, '$\{x: Fx\} \epsilon y$'. Instead of saying this we could say that $z \epsilon y$ for something z which is, in fact, the set $\{x: Fx\}$; and to say that z is $\{x: Fx\}$ is the work of a moment: $(x)(x \epsilon z . \equiv Fx)$. Thus the context '$\{x: Fx\} \epsilon y$' of the term '$\{x: Fx\}$' is paraphrased as follows:

$$\exists z \, (z \, \epsilon \, y \, . \, \forall x \, (x \, \epsilon \, z \, . \, \equiv \, Fx) \,).$$

Similarly for other immediate contexts of the term '$\{x: Fx\}$'. Once we have accounted thus for terms of abstraction in all desired contexts, we can explain many further familiar notations of set theory as abbreviations of terms of abstraction: thus the complement $\bar{y}$ is $\{x: \sim(x \epsilon y)\}$, the intersection $y \cap z$ is $\{x: x \epsilon y . x \epsilon z\}$, the union $y \cup z$ is $\{x: x \epsilon y \text{ or } x \epsilon z\}$, the empty set Λ is $\{x: \sim(x = x) \}$, the unit set $\{y\}$ is $\{x: x = y\}$, and the set $\{y, z\}$ is $\{y\} \cup \{z\}$.

It was remarked late in Chapter 3 that set theories are many, differing not just in formulation but in content: in respect of what sets are said to exist. It can happen, among these variations, that a set theory is propounded that is after all not wholly translatable into standard form with 'ϵ' as sole predicate. Usually, however, this basis suffices, and we do well to cleave to it when we can rather than choosing to define 'ϵ' and the logical signs on the basis of other notations. The advantage is standardization, and hence ease in comparing the various systems of set theory with one another.

Pioneers in modern logic viewed set theory as logic; thus Frege, Peano, and various of their followers, notably Whitehead and Russell. Frege, Whitehead, and Russell made a point of reducing mathematics to logic; Frege claimed in 1884 to have proved in this way, contrary to Kant, that the truths of arithmetic are analytic. But the logic capable of encompassing this reduction was logic inclusive of set theory.

Set theory in sheep's clothing   This tendency to see set theory as logic has depended early and late on overestimating the kinship between membership and predication. An intermediate notion, attribution of attributes, insinuates itself and heightens the illusion of continuity.

In the innocent 'Fx' of the logic of quantification, the schematic letter 'F' stands in place of a predicate. Or, more explicitly, the combination 'Fx' stands in the place of an open sentence in 'x'; whether the sentence has 'x' on one side and an isolated predicate on the other is of no moment. What is important is that in writing 'F' and 'Fx' we are just schematically simulating sentences and their parts; we are not *referring* to predicates or other strings of signs, nor are we referring to attributes or sets. Some logicians, however, have taken a contrary line, reading 'F' as an attribute variable and 'Fx' as 'x has F'. Some, fond of attributes, have done this with their eyes open; others have been seduced into it by a confusion.

The confusion begins as a confusion of sign and object; a confusion between mentioning a sign and using it. Instead of seeing 'F' steadfastly as *standing in place of* an unspecified predicate, our confused logician sees it half the time as *naming* an unspecified predicate. Thus 'F' gains noun status, enabling him to read 'Fx' as 'x has F' without offending his grammatical ear. Having got this far, he can round out his confusion by calling F an attribute. This attunes his usage to that of the unconfused but prodigal logician who embraces attributes with his eyes open.

The prodigal logician is identifiable with Frege. The confused logician could be Russell, despite his great contributions.

The quantifiers '$\exists F$' and '$\forall F$' are at the heart of the matter. I already deplored this sort of quantification somewhat after the middle of Chapter 2. I think it worth while now to develop my objections in more detail.

Consider first some ordinary quantifications: '$\exists x$ (x walks)', '$\forall x$ (x walks), '$\exists x$ (x is prime)'. The open sentence after the quantifier shows 'x' in a position where a name could stand; a name of a walker, for instance, or of a prime number. The quantifications do not mean that names walk or are prime; what are said to walk or to be prime are things that could be named *by* names in those positions. To put the predicate letter 'F' in a quantifier, then, is to treat predicate positions suddenly as name positions, and hence to treat predicates as names of entities of some sort. The quantifier '$\exists F$' or '$\forall F$' says not that some or all predicates are thus and so, but that some or all entities of the sort named by predicates are thus and so. The logician who grasps this point, and still quantifies 'F', may say that these entities are attributes; attributes are for him the values of 'F', the things over which 'F' ranges. The more confused logician, on the other hand, may say that these entities, the values of 'F', are predicates. He fails to appreciate the difference between schematically *simulating* predicates and quantificationally talking *about* predicates, let alone talking about attributes.

Even the first logician's line here is to be deplored. I urged in Chapter 1 that propositions are undesirable; and the same goes for attributes. Attributes are to predicates, or open sentences, as propositions are to closed sentences. Attributes are like propositions in the inadequacy of their individuation. Sets are well individuated by the *law of extensionality*, which identifies sets whose members are the same; but this law fails for attributes, save as the word 'attribute' is ill-applied and 'set' would serve better. Open sentences that are true of just the same things never determine two sets, but may determine two attributes. What is further required for sameness of attributes is synonymy, in some sense, of the open sentences; and in Chapter 1 we despaired of making satisfactory sense of such synonymy.

Some logicians, for this reason, view the values of 'F' as sets. But I deplore the use of predicate letters as quantified variables, even when the values are sets. Predicates have attributes as their "intensions" or meanings (or would if there were attributes), and they have sets as their extensions; but they are names of neither. Variables eligible for quantification therefore do not belong in predicate positions. They belong in name positions.

To put the point another way: even one who admits attributes should not read 'Fx' as 'x has F', with 'F' thus in name position; rather let him write 'x has y', or, if he prefers distinctive variables for attributes, 'x has ζ'. Likewise, if someone wants to admit sets as values of quantifiable variables, let him write '$x \in y$'; or, if he prefers distinctive variables for sets, '$x \in \alpha$'. Let him switch explicitly to what I called in Chapter 4 the set-theoretic analogue. The predicate letter 'F', like the sentence letter 'p', is not a value-taking variable at all, but just a substitution-taking schematic letter.

If anyone thought attributes a more congenial assumption than sets, he could assume quantification over attributes and then introduce quantification over sets, or a reasonable facsimile, by a certain scheme of contextual definition. Russell took this line. The point of the definition is just to secure the law of extensionality for sets without assuming it for attributes; for this law is the only difference between the two domains. But why would Russell find attributes a more congenial assumption than sets? It was a case rather of not appreciating where elementary logic, in its innocent simulation of predicates, gave way to talk about attributes. The phrase 'propositional function', adapted from Frege, cloaked the confusion; Russell used it to refer sometimes to predicates and sometimes to attributes. As a result it was thought by some that Russell had derived set theory, and therewith mathematics generally, from narrowly logical beginnings.

Followers of Hilbert have continued to quantify predicate letters, obtaining what they call a higher-order predicate calculus. The values of these variables are in effect sets; and this way of presenting set theory gives it a deceptive resemblance to logic. One is apt to feel that no abrupt addition to the ordinary logic of quantification has been made; just some more quantifiers, governing predicate letters already present. In order to appreciate how deceptive this line can be, consider the hypothesis '$\exists y \, \forall x \, (x \in y \, . \, \leftrightarrow Fx)$'. It assumes a set $\{x \colon Fx\}$ determined by an open sentence in the role of 'Fx'. This is the central hypothesis of set theory, and the one that has to be restrained in one way or another to avoid the paradoxes. This hypothesis itself falls out of sight in the so-called higher-order predicate calculus. We get '$\exists G \, \forall x \, (Gx \leftrightarrow Fx)$', which evidently follows from the genuinely logical triviality '$\forall x \, (Fx \leftrightarrow Fx)$' by an elementary logical inference. There is no actual risk of paradox as long as the ranges of values of 'x' and 'G' are kept apart, but still a fair bit of set theory has slipped in unheralded.

Logic in wolf's clothing   The set theorist's ontological excesses may sometimes escape public notice, we see, disguised as logic. But we must in fairness recognize also an opposite tendency, toward over-acknowledgement: a tendency to speak ostensibly of sets or attributes where logic in a narrower sense would have sufficed. This tendency is evident even in everyday discourse, where it serves a purpose of abbreviative cross-reference. To save repeating a sentence, unchanged except for some proper name, one says "The same applies to Eisenhower." If it crossed one's minds to ask "The same what?" one might answer "The same attribute." Or again one may say that it is a trait or attribute or property of a born seaman never to quail at the fury of the gale, when all one means is that a born seaman never quails at the fury of the gale. These ostensible references to attributes make no capital of attributes as objects, and are easily paraphrased away.

Some of what is done in the name of set theory, similarly, is quite within the reach of elementary logic. This is true in particular of what they call set theory in the "new math." The Boolean algebra of unions, intersections, and complements merely does in another notation what can be done in that part of the logic of quantification which uses only one-place predicate letters. The variables in Boolean algebra are unquantified and can be read as schematic one-place predicate letters.

There is something to be said, however, for pressing this sham invocation of sets. We can in this way enjoy the convenience of an ontology of sets, up to a point, without footing the ontological bill; we can explain the sham sets away as a mere manner of speaking, by contextual definition, when the ontological reckoning comes. To whatever degree such an effort succeeds—to whatever degree we gain the utility of sets on this cost-free basis—to that degree we weaken the pragmatic case for an ontology of sets. Actually we cannot thus succeed in showing such an ontology superfluous in the end; but we can show it superfluous for some purposes that might have been thought to require it, and for other purposes we can perhaps show that a more modest ontology of sets will suffice than one might have thought.

The key definition contextually defines membership and abstraction together, in the combination '$y \epsilon \{ x: Fx \}$'. The method of contextual definition which we already noted a few pages back would explain this combination as short for:

$$(4) \qquad \exists z \, (y \, \epsilon \, z \, . \, \forall x \, (x \, \epsilon \, z \, . \, \leftrightarrow Fx) \,),$$

and this would be all right in an honest set theory; but it is useless to our new project of simulation, for two reasons. In the first place, if behind our simulation we would like to maintain that there are in fact no sets, then (4), which affirms the existence of a set z, would come out false for all choices of y and for all sentences in the role of 'Fx'. The combination '$y \epsilon \{ x: Fx \}$' thus defined would be indiscriminately false and thus useless. In the second place, the formula (4) already uses the predicate 'ϵ', whereas we want rather to simulate the apparatus of set theory on the basis of an object language lacking that apparatus.

So we need another definition of the combination '$y \epsilon \{ x:$

Fx }'. Let us seek no farther; '*Fy*' will do. We simply agree to write '*y* ε {*x: Fx* }' at will in place of '*Fy*', for each object *y* and each open sentence in place of '*Fy*'.[1]

We would also like a contextual definition for the combination '{*x: Fx* } ε *y*', but this wish will remain unfulfilled. Such is the limit of our simulation. We do only what we can by means of the combination '*y* ε {*x: Fx* }'.

Scope of the virtual theory   Immediately we may proceed to define the familiar notations '{*z* }', '{*z, z'* }', and '∧' as '{*x: x = z* }', '{*x: x = z* or *x = z'* }', and '{*x: ~(x = x)* }'; also 'V', for the universal set, as '{*x: x = x* }'. But of course these definitions provide for the notations '{*z* }', '{*z, z'* }', '∧', and 'V' only in positions after 'ε'.

To facilitate the further exposition of this simulation let us adopt the letters '*α*', '*β*', etc., as schematic letters for the positions of *abstracts*, that is, terms of the form '{*x: Fx* }'. Being schematic, these letters are not quantifiable variables. Then we proceed with the obvious definitions of the notations of the Boolean algebra of sets:

$$'\bar{\alpha}' \text{ for } '\{x: \sim(x \,\epsilon\, \alpha) \}',$$
$$'\alpha \cap \beta' \text{ for } '\{x: x \,\epsilon\, \alpha \,.\, x \,\epsilon\, \beta\}'$$
$$'\alpha \cup \beta' \text{ for } '\{x: x \,\epsilon\, \alpha \text{ or } x \,\epsilon\, \beta\}',$$
$$'\alpha \subseteq \beta' \text{ for } '\sim\exists x \,(x \,\epsilon\, \alpha \,.\, \sim (x \,\epsilon\, \beta) \,)'.$$

We are imagining, beneath these definitions, some standard object language with its lexicon of predicates. In availing myself of the identity sign in my definitions of '{*z* }', '{*z, z'* }', '∧', and 'V', just now; I imagined '*x = y*' to have been defined in terms of the predicates of the object language in the way that was illustrated in (3) early in this chapter. Now '=' so defined is defined for use only between variables, not between abstracts (or between '*α*' and '*β*'). Independently, however, we can easily define '=' between abstracts. Since all occurrences of abstracts reduce to occurrences after 'ε', the same idea that led to (3) automatically delivers '∀*x* (*x* ε *α* .↔. *x* ε *β*)' as the definition of '*α = β*'. Equivalently, if we exploit the inclusion sign '⊆' last previously defined, '*α = β*' comes to '*α ⊆ β . β ⊆ α*'. The identity '{*x: Fx*} = {*x: Gx*}' boils down to '∀*x* (*Fx* ↔ *Gx*)'.

It is time for a word concerning the pair of terms 'set 'and 'class'. They were interchangeable until, in recent decades, this superfluity of terms was put to good use in marking a technical distinction.

---

[1] The convention calls for certain technical refinements, passed over here. See my *Set Theory and Its Logic*, pp. 16f.

Some set theories avoid the paradoxes by declaring some classes not to be members of anything. The word 'set' is thereupon reserved for the narrower sense: classes that are members. The others I call *ultimate* classes. For set theories without ultimate classes, 'set' and 'class' continue to be interchangeable.

Now our definition of '$y \in \{x: Fx\}$' as 'Fy' gives us a simulation not so much of sets as of ultimate classes; for it makes no provision for an abstraction expression '$\{x: Fx\}$' to the left of '$\in$'. For this reason I call the simulation the *virtual theory of classes*, or the theory of virtual classes; not of sets. But note still that the procedure only simulates; it does not provide for genuine classes. For even an ultimate class $\{x: Fx\}$, if it were really assumed and not just simulated, would be assumed as a value of the variables of quantification. We would be able to say that $\exists z\ (z = \{x: Fx\})$; also we would be able to apply any generality of the form '$\forall z\ Gz$' to '$\{x: Fx\}$' so as to infer that $G\{x: Fx\}$. Our definition makes no sense of such moves.

Suppose the object language really talks nowhere of classes; '$\in$' is not in its lexicon and there are only individuals, no classes, in its universe. Then the virtual theory of classes, superimposed on the object language, has the effect of simulating classes of individuals. It simulates them up to a point, just short of quantifying over them. But it does not at all simulate classes of classes, classes of sets. In particular, therefore, it stops short of ordered pairs. The usual way of accommodating relations in set theory, namely as classes of pairs, is thus out of reach.

We can, however, simulate relations by a definition parallel to our definition of '$y \in \{x: Fx\}$'. We can contextually define a notation '$\{xx': Fxx'\}$' of abstraction of relations, purporting to name the relation of each thing x to each thing x' such that Fxx'. We define '$\{xx': Fxx'\}$' in the 'bears' context; that is, we say what it means for y to bear $\{xx': Fxx'\}$ to y'; namely, of course, Fyy'. A virtual theory of relations, far more elaborate than that of classes, can be developed on this basis.[1]

There is much that we can derive from genuine set theory that we cannot derive from these flimsy simulations of classes and relations. If, however, contrary to the supposition of the preceding paragraph but one, we let the object language have an '$\in$' in its lexicon and a modest provision of real classes in its universe, we can still get

---

[1] For an extended treatment of the virtual theory of classes and relations, and reference to earlier work by R. M. Martin and others, see my *Set Theory and Its Logic*, §§ 2–3.

a little additional mileage by superimposing the virtual theory to get virtual classes and relations of real classes.

We saw earlier in this chapter that the boundary between logic and set theory can become very much obscured. It was in order to adduce further evidence to that same effect that I wanted to sketch the virtual theory of classes and relations in these pages. But I do not want thereby to suggest that the boundary is a minor one, or a vague one. On the contrary, I think it important and worth clarifying.

The virtual theory of classes and relations is indeed logic, pure logic in disguise. But as soon as we admit 'ϵ' as a genuine predicate, and classes as values of quantifiable variables, we are embarked on a substantive mathematical theory. We are out beyond the reach of complete proof procedures, and in a domain even of competing doctrines. It is no defect of the structural versions of logical truth that they exclude genuine set theory from the field of logic.

Simulated class quantification   We were drawn to our study of the simulation of objects by an interest in the status of set theory. Simulated set theory is logic; real set theory is not. The simulation of objects is of interest also apart from this question, however, and of interest also for domains other than set theory. Let us pursue it a little further.

When we take on set theory forthrightly and without simulation, we take on both vocabulary and ontology. We let 'ϵ' into our lexicon and classes into the range of values of our variables. When, on the other hand, we simulate set theory by a virtual theory, we simulate the lexical addendum 'ϵ' by contextual definition. On the ontological side our simulation is feebler; we adopt schematic class letters that suggest variables, but we do not quantify them.

The idea suggests itself of improving the counterfeit by simulating quantification over the simulated objects. Any further set-theoretic strength that we could borrow in this way, beyond what was already afforded by the virtual theory, would be a further philosophical bargain. The contextual definitions would still excuse the whole notation as a mere manner of speaking, eliminable on demand.

There are sorts of limited quantification that can indeed be contextually defined. Suppose the one-place predicates in the lexicon of our object language are a mere hundred in number: 'P_0', 'P_1', ..., 'P_{99}'. As stressed a little earlier, these are not names. Their positions are not positions for quantified variables. Still, by contextual definition we can introduce a new style of quantified variable, say 'a',

'β', etc., expressly for those positions. For, take any sentence, however complex, containing say the predicate 'P_0' at one or more points. Picture the sentence as '$—— P_0 ——$'. Now we can explain the new existential quantification '$\exists \alpha\ (—— \alpha ——)$' as short for a hundred-fold alternation:

$$——P_0—— \text{ or } ——P_1—— \text{ or } \ldots \text{ or } ——P_{99}——.$$

Correspondingly '$(\alpha)\ (—— \alpha ——)$' is short for a hundred-fold conjunction. In this way the hundred predicates become, purely in a manner of speaking, names each of a new fictitious object, a pretended value of the new variable 'α' of quantification. We may adopt this convention of abbreviation for each choice of sentence in the role of '$—— P_0 ——$' and each of the variables in place of 'α'. Predicates have become names after all; but only in a manner of speaking, to be paraphrased away at will.

A hundred fictitious new objects thus accrue, or fewer if two predicates are taken to be names of the same new object. But this latter choice is excluded unless, to begin with, the two predicates were coextensive: true of just the same things. For, as long as there is something x such that $P_i x$ and $\sim P_j x$, we shall not want the two predicates to name the same value of 'α'; we shall not want that αx and $\sim \alpha x$.

Even if there are coextensive predicates among the hundred, could we still insist upon a full hundred fictitious objects, all different, for them to name? Not more, of course; we would not want one predicate to stand ambiguously as the name of two. But why not a full hundred, thus letting coextensive predicates name different objects? This question revives a distinction noted a little earlier: the difference between viewing predicates as naming attributes and as naming classes. Do we want these new objects, newly named by the hundred predicates, to be attributes or to be classes?

It is of course just a question of how to define our new equations '$P_i = P_j$', or '$\alpha = \beta$'. The ordinary '$x = y$' may be supposed already defined in the style, still, of (3); but definition of '$=$' between predicates, in their new semblance of names, is a further step. Presumably it will consist in explaining '$P_i = P_j$' as short for some long sentence S_{ij} containing these two predicates; for each two predicates that sentence will be the same, except for i and j; and in particular S_{ii} will come out true. If this much is granted, then our question ('May coextensive predicates name different objects?') receives a negative answer, as follows.

Our object language has, we suppose, the standard grammar (Chapter 2). But any such language is *extensional*; that is, coextensive predicates are interchangeable *salva veritate*.[1] No true sentence in the language can become false when an occurrence of a predicate is supplanted by a coextensive predicate. So, suppose 'P_i' and 'P_j' coextensive; then, since S_{ii} is true, S_{ij} will be true. In short, '$P_i = P_j$' will hold for coextensive 'P_i' and 'P_j'. The fictitious objects named by the predicates thus behave as classes rather than attributes.

The triviality of this simulation is its finitude: there are just the hundred or fewer fictitious classes. This is why we were able to resort to alternation and conjunction in defining '$(\exists\alpha)$' and '(α)'. By complicating the definitions we could accommodate, as further ostensible values of variables, all the classes that can be got from these hundred or fewer by Boolean intersection, union, and complement or various other operations; and the reason is that they too will still be finite in number. But let us not pause over them. Instead let us turn to a different and yet more trivial example of contextually defined quantification over fictitious objects.

Other simulated quantification   Sentences are not names. Their positions are not positions for quantified variables. Still, by contextual definition we can very easily introduce a new style of quantified variable, say 'p', 'q', etc., expressly for those positions. For, take a compound sentence and put the letter 'p' in the place of a closed constituent sentence. Let us picture the result as '—— p ——.' We want to define the new quantification '$\forall p$ (—— p ——)' in such a way that it will count as true, once and for all, if and only if the expression '—— p ——' comes out true under all substitutions of closed sentences for the letter 'p'. In order to see how to formulate such a definition, let us reflect once more on the extensional character of our object language. What this means for closed sentences is simply that all the true ones are interchangeable in all contexts *salva veritate* and all the false ones are too. It follows that the expression '—— p ——' will become true under *all* substitutions for 'p' so long merely as it becomes true under *two*: the substitution of some true sentence and some false one. Therefore we can define the quantification '$\forall p$ (—— p ——)' simply as the conjunction:

$$\text{——}\exists x\, P_0x\text{——}\ .\ \text{——}{\sim}\ \exists x\, P_0x\text{——},$$

---

[1] The proof is again substantially § 18 of *Mathematical Logic*.

where the closed sentence '$\exists x\, P_0 x$' is adopted arbitrarily. We can define the existential quantification '$\exists p\, (— — p — —)$' in parallel fashion:

$$— — \exists x\, P_0 x — —\ \text{or}\ — — —\,\sim\exists x\, P_0 x — —.$$

In this way the closed sentences become, purely in a manner of speaking, names each of a new fictitious object, a pretended value of the new variable 'p' of quantification. These objects may be identified with the truth values; the truths name one of them and the falsehoods the other. The notion of sentences as names of truth values, which goes back to Frege, is thus reconstituted as an eliminable manner of speaking.

For the next example, a more substantial one, suppose as a starting point an object language of elementary number theory. It has notation for the truth functions and quantification and, let us suppose, the identity predicate and the addition and multiplication functors (though strictly, for standard grammar, these would be reduced to other predicates as remarked in Chapter 2). The values of the variables are just the positive integers. but we can introduce the fractional notation 'x/y' for ratios by contextual definition, as follows:

$$\begin{aligned}
&\text{'}x = y/z\text{' and '}y/z = x\text{' for '}y = x{\cdot}z\text{',}\\
&\text{'}x/y = z/w\text{' for '}x{\cdot}w = y{\cdot}z\text{',}\\
&\text{'}x + y/z\text{' and '}y/z + x\text{' for '}(x{\cdot}z + y)/z\text{',}\\
&\text{'}x/y + z/w\text{' for '}(x{\cdot}w + y{\cdot}z)/(y{\cdot}w)\text{',}\\
&\text{'}x{\cdot}(y/z)\text{' and '}(y/z){\cdot}x\text{' for '}(x{\cdot}y)/z\text{',}\\
&\text{'}(x/y){\cdot}(z/w)\text{' for '}(x{\cdot}z)/(y{\cdot}w)\text{'.}
\end{aligned}$$

Note that all the explanations at the right are expressed in terms of the arithmetic of integers, or else reduce to those terms by means of the intervening definitions.

It will be found that any equation that talks of sums and products of ratios, or of ratios and integers mixed, can be paraphrased step by step according to the above contextual definitions until finally it talks only of sums and products of integers. We thus have what might be called a virtual theory of ratios; and thus far no quantification over ratios. But the further step to a contextually defined quantification over ratios is now easy. To say that something holds for all (or some) ratios r is just to say that, for all (or some) integers x and y, it holds for x/y. We move in this way from the elementary theory of positive integers to the full elementary theory of positive ratios without adding anything but manners of speaking. The ratios enter purely as fictitious new numbers, but they enter in full quantified force.

Unlike our two preceding examples of the contextual definition of quantification over fictitious new objects, this one affords quantification over infinitely many. What made it possible, however, is still finitude in a relative sense: each of the infinitely many new objects x/y is determined by finitely many of the old ones, in fact two.

The pleasure one takes in this cost-free extension of the domain of elementary number theory is diminished when one reflects that it is also possible, by methods that I shall not here enlarge upon, to reinterpret the elementary theory of ratios within elementary number theory unaided by newly defined quantification. This situation is characteristic. Contextual definition of simulated quantification over simulated objects is in general an unproductive recreation.

Annexes   The last definition of logical truth in Chapter 4 had an appealing generality. It coincided with the others in application to object languages of the contemplated sort, but it made interesting sense also in application to languages with other than standard grammar. It counted a sentence logically true when all sentences are true that share its grammatical structure. Let us now consider how this widened conception of logical truth works out when the standard grammar is supplemented in certain seemingly needed ways.

The adequacy of our standard grammar already came into question late in Chapter 2, on the score of adverbs. We considered adding a grammatical category comprising adverbs, and adding also a grammatical construction which would take a predicate and an adverb as its constituents and produce a complex predicate. Thereupon the sentence:

$$(5) \qquad \sim\exists x \, (x \text{ walks rapidly.} \sim(x \text{ walks})),$$

or 'Whatever walks rapidly walks', would qualify as logically true under the broader definition that reckons logical truth by full grammatical structure, though not under the definition that limits attention to truth functions and quantification. This example does credit to the broader definition.

The schemata that facilitate the formal study of logic would need supplementing, to cover cases like (5). Letters of some distinctive style would be adopted as schematic letters for adverbs, and a notation would be adopted for joining adverb to predicate. Proof precedures would be devised that would generate valid schemata of the new kind—among them a schema depicting the structure of (5).

The added category of adverbs might contain complex adverbs, compounded by further grammatical constructions. There might be a construction generating adverbs from predicates—thus 'rapidly' from '(is) rapid'. The broad definition that reckons logical truth by full grammatical structure would then recruit yet further logical truths, all perhaps as deserving of the title as (5) was. A further supplementation of schematic notation and proof procedure would follow along.

All this supplementary logical apparatus for adverbs becomes superfluous if we can see our way to doing the work of the adverbs by some devious plan, Davidson's or another, within the bounds of standard grammar. A comparable benefit was already conferred by the four-dimensional view, in its elimination of tense; we were thereby spared the cumbersome triviality of a logic of tenses. Reduction to standard grammar is reduction to standard logic, the neat and efficient logic of truth functions and quantification that we understand so well. When we paraphrase a theory into standard form we are, in effect, programming our standard logical computer to deal with the logical problems of the theory.

Another seemingly supplementary branch of logic has been brought to my attention by Peter Geach: the logic of comparatives. One's first thought is that the suffix 'er' attaches to a one-place predicate to yield a two-place predicate subject to the logical laws:

$$(6) \qquad \sim\exists x \ F_{er}xx,$$

$$(7) \qquad \sim\exists x \ \exists y \ \exists z \ (F_{er}xy \ . \ F_{er}yz \ . \ \sim F_{er}xz).$$

However, there is a semantic difficulty. A predicate resists the comparative suffix except insofar as it is systematically vague or elliptical to begin with, gaining precision only in the comparative. For instance the two-place predicates 'is bigger than' and 'is heavier than' are quite in order, but what is simply big or heavy? In a logically well-regimented language 'is bigger than' would figure as a simple two-place predicate, and then the positive 'is big', where useful, would be paraphrased as 'is bigger than' followed by a reference to some object chosen as a minimum standard suitable for the purposes at hand. The suffix 'er' would be seen thus not as a particle signalling a construction, but just as a syllable occurring in certain simple two-place predicates and reserved, as it happens, to predicates fulfilling the irreflexivity and transitivity conditions (6) and (7).

The superlative raises no separate problem, being in principle superfluous. '$F_{est}x$' can be paraphrased thus:

$$\exists y \, F_{er}xy \, . \sim \exists y \, F_{er}yx.$$

There was some forlorn talk, late in Chapter 2, of the idioms of propositional attitude and modality. We noted that these idioms cause sentences to be constituents of constructions other than truth functions and quantifications. A consequence is that extensionality lapses; coextensive predicates cease to be interchangeable. There is no absurdity in this lapse, but it is calculated to complicate logical theory. A graver threat, noted late in Chapter 2, is the failure of interchangeability even of the terms of an identity, 'Cicero = Tully'. This failure contravenes the very meaning of identity, unless it happens in places where the names do not serve merely to refer to their objects. Strictly speaking of course the failure will not appear in this form as long as we dispense with names; but, as hinted late in Chapter 2, it takes a subtler form having to do with variables.

In those pages we stopped short of the special grammatical apparatus that might be called forth by such questions of identity and variables. Adhering to broader lines, though, we did contrast three ways of organizing the grammar of propositional attitudes. One way recognized a construction of names from sentences; one way recognized a construction of one-place predicates from two-place predicates and sentences; and one way recognized a construction of one-place predicates from attitudinatives and sentences. Each of these three choices would call forth, under our widened conception of logical truth, a distinctive supplementation of the schematic notations of logic.

It is instructive at this point to mention yet a fourth conceivable way of organizing the grammar of propositional attitudes. Since the required vocabulary of attitudinatives is small, we might discard that lexical category and treat each attitudinative rather as a particle signaling a distinctive construction: always a construction that takes a sentence as its constituent and delivers a one-place predicate. One of these would be the belief construction, delivering predicates of the form 'believes that p'; another would be the wishing construction; and so on. On this approach, 'believes that' and 'wishes that' would find their way into the eventual logical schemata on a par with their austerer predecessors '$\sim$', '$.$', '$\exists x$'.

Somehow such an outcome does not seem suitable. Logically the attitudinatives 'believes that' and 'wishes that' seem too colorful to count as pure logical particles. But on the grammatical side one feels equally that the attitudinatives are too colorful to count as grammatical particles; they belong in the lexicon. These intuitions, for all their vagueness, match up. I see here further support for our abstract definition of logical truth by reference to grammatical structure.

Let us put aside this bizarre fourth way of organizing the grammar of the propositional attitudes. The three others remain. Whichever is chosen, the outcome is a rather heavy supplementation of grammar along with a curiously poor supplementation of logic. We get new schemata, yes: perhaps schemata containing such clauses as 'Fx(that p)', where 'F' stands in place of some two-place predicate like 'believes'. But what such schema can we point to as valid? On this score the modalities are more productive. We get, among others, the valid schema '$\sim(\sim p$. necessarily $p)$'. Also from every valid schema, e.g. 'p or $\sim p$', we get another by applying 'necessarily'; thus 'necessarily $(p$ or $\sim p)$'.

If some of the burden of the idioms of propositional attitude can someday be taken over by a clearer conceptual apparatus, an incidental gain may prove to be that some laws emerge appropriate to the subject. One outcome, and a happy one, of course might be that the needs could be met by skillful padding of lexicon and ontology, without exceeding the bounds of standard grammar. In this case the laws that emerged would not count as logic.

The rewards of staying within the bounds of standard grammar are great. There is extensionality, lately remarked upon. There is, more generally speaking, the efficiency and elegance of the logic of truth functions and quantification. There is its completeness ((B) of Chapter 4), whereof more in Chapter 6. There is the impressive concurrence of all those definitions of logical truth in Chapter 4; they all proved to demarcate one and the same class of sentences, as long as we adhere to standard grammar and allow ourselves a fairly robust vocabulary. There is a concurrence here that suggests we have hold of something solid and significant.

DEVIANT LOGICS

6

Change
of logic,
change of
subject In the preceding chapter we discussed the bounds of logic. We considered where, within the totality of science that we accept, the reasonable boundary falls between what we may best call logic and what we may best call something else. We considered also, outside the firm area thus bounded, certain supplementary developments which we would include under the name of logic if we were to admit them into our total science at all. We did not consider any possible inroads on the firm area itself. This is our next topic: the possible abrogation of the orthodox logic of truth functions or of quantification in favor of some deviant logic.

The systems of orthodox logic are themselves many and varied. The differences among them are not such as make deviant logics. It is one logic variously expounded and variously serviced by computers or proof procedures. Demarcate the totality of logical truths, in whatever terms, and you have in those terms specified the logic. Which of these truths one chooses to designate as axioms, and what rules he devises for generating the rest of the logical truths from those axioms, is indifferent. Whether he elects the axiomatic style at all, or some other sort of proof procedure, or none, is again indifferent. The kind of deviation now to be considered, on the other hand, is of a more substantial kind. It is not just a change of methods of generating the class of logical truths, but a change of that class itself. It is not just a change of demarcation, either, between what to call logical truth and what to call extra-logical truth. It is a question rather of outright rejection of part of our logic as not true at all.

It would seem that such an idea of deviation in logic is absurd on the face of it. If sheer logic is not conclusive, what is? What higher tribunal could abrogate the logic of truth functions or of quantification?

Suppose someone were to propound a heterodox logic in which all the laws which have up to now been taken to govern alternation were made to govern conjunction instead, and vice versa. Clearly we would regard his deviation merely as notational and phonetic. For obscure reasons, if any, he has taken to writing 'and' in place of 'or' and vice versa. We impute our orthodox logic to him, or impose it upon him, by translating his deviant dialect.

Could we be wrong in so doing? Could he really be meaning and thinking genuine conjunction in his use of 'and' after all, just as we do, and genuine alternation in his use of 'or', and merely disagreeing with us on points of logical doctrine respecting the laws of conjunction and alternation? Clearly this is nonsense. There is no residual essence of conjunction and alternation in addition to the sounds and notations and the laws in conformity with which a man uses those sounds and notations.

To turn to a popular extravaganza, what if someone were to reject the law of non-contradication and so accept an occasional sentence and its negation both as true? An answer one hears is that this would vitiate all science. Any conjunction of the form 'p . $\sim p$' logically implies every sentence whatever; therefore acceptance of one sentence and its negation as true would commit us to accepting every sentence as true, and thus forfeiting all distinction between true and false.

In answer to this answer, one hears that such a full-width trivialization could perhaps be staved off by making compensatory adjustments to block this indiscriminate deducibility of all sentences from an inconsistency. Perhaps, it is suggested, we can so rig our new logic that it will isolate its contradictions and contain them.

My view of this dialogue is that neither party knows what he is talking about. They think they are talking about negation, '$\sim$', 'not'; but surely the notation ceased to be recognizable as negation when they took to regarding some conjunctions of the form 'p . $\sim p$' as true, and stopped regarding such sentences as implying all others. Here, evidently, is the deviant logician's predicament: when he tries to deny the doctrine he only changes the subject.

Take the less fanciful case of trying to construe some unknown
language on the strength of observable behavior. If a native is
prepared to assent to some compound sentence but not to a
constituent, this is a reason not to construe the construction as conjunction. If a native is prepared to assent to a constituent but not to
the compound, this is a reason not to construe the construction as
alternation. We impute our orthodox logic to him, or impose it on
him, by translating his language to suit. We build the logic into our
manual of translation. Nor is there cause here for apology. We have
to base translation on some kind of evidence, and what better?

Being thus built into translation is not an exclusive trait of
logic. If the natives are not prepared to assent to a certain sentence
in the rain, then equally we have reason not to translate the sentence
as 'It is raining'. Naturally the native's unreadiness to assent to a
certain sentence gives us reason not to construe the sentence as saying something whose truth should be obvious to the native at the
time. Data of this sort are all we have to go on when we try to
decipher a language on the basis of verbal behavior in observable
circumstances.

Still, logic is built into translation more fully than other systematic departments of science. It is in the incidence of obviousness
that the difference lies. Preparatory to developing this point I must
stress that I am using the word 'obvious' in an ordinary behavioral
sense, with no epistemological overtones. When I call '1 + 1 = 2'
obvious to a community I mean only that everyone, nearly enough,
will unhesitatingly assent to it, for whatever reason; and when I call
'It is raining' obvious in particular circumstances I mean that everyone will assent to it in those circumstances.

It behooves us, in construing a strange language, to make the
obvious sentences go over into English sentences that are true and,
preferably, also obvious; this is the point we have been noting. Now
this canon—'Save the obvious'—is sufficient to settle, in point of
truth value anyway, our translations of *some* of the sentences in just
about every little branch of knowledge or discourse; for some of
them are pretty sure to qualify as obvious outright (like '1 + 1 = 2')
or obvious in particular circumstances (like 'It is raining'). At the
same time, just about every little branch of knowledge or discourse
will contain other sentences which are not thus guaranteed true by
translation, not being obvious.

But on this score logic is peculiar: every logical truth is obvious,
actually or potentially. Each, that is to say, is either obvious as it
stands or can be reached from obvious truths by a sequence of indi-

vidually obvious steps. To say this is in effect just to repeat some remarks of Chapter 4: that the logic of quantification and identity admits of complete proof procedures, and some of these are procedures that generate sentences purely from visibly true sentences by steps that visibly preserve truth.

In a negative sense, consequently, logical truth is guaranteed under translation. The canon 'Save the obvious' bans any manual of translation that would represent the foreigners as contradicting our logic (apart perhaps from corrigible confusions in complex sentences). What is negative about this guarantee is that it does not assure that all our logically true sentences carry over into truths of the foreign language; some of them might resist translation altogether.

The law of excluded middle
One issue that calls for examination under the head of deviant logic has to do with the law of excluded middle, or *tertium non datur*. This law, which has been contested in some quarters, may be pictured variously:

(1) Every closed sentence is true or false,
(2) Every closed sentence or its negation is true,
(3) Every closed sentence is true or not true.

We may as well economize on components by explaining falsity as truth of the negation. This reduces (1) to (2). As for (3), it looks more modest than (2). What little it affirms continues to hold, unlike (2), even when we change 'closed sentence' to 'open sentence' or 'question' or 'command' and even when we change 'true' to 'brief' or 'musical'. The form of (3) is '$\forall x$ (if Fx then Gx or $\sim Gx$)', whose validity follows from that of 'p or $\sim p$'. Still, what does it mean to call 'p or $\sim p$' valid? Simply that it comes out true with any closed sentence in place of 'p'. But this amounts in effect to (2), it would seem, after all, so that the difference in strength between (2) and (3) is illusory. Schematically, the law of excluded middle is simply 'p or $\sim p$'.

These trivial latter lucubrations well illustrate the inanity of trying to discern equivalence in some sense within the domain of logical truth. Logical equivalence, as of Chapter 4, holds indiscriminately between all logical truths.

By the reasoning of a couple of pages back, whoever denies the law of excluded middle changes the subject. This is not to say that he is wrong in so doing. In repudiating 'p or $\sim p$' he is indeed giving up classical negation, or perhaps alternation, or both; and he may have his reasons.

One setting where classical negation and alternation fall away is many-valued logic. This kind of logic was developed somewhat by C. S. Peirce in the last century, and independently later by Łukasiewicz. It is like the logic of truth functions except that it recognizes three or more so-called truth values instead of truth and falsity. Primarily the motivation of these studies has been abstractly mathematical: the pursuit of analogy and generalization. Studied in this spirit, many-valued logic is logic only analogically speaking; it is uninterpreted theory, abstract algebra.

Sometimes, however, three-valued logic is envisaged as an improved logic. Its three values are called truth, falsity, and something intermediate. A construction called negation carries so-called truths into falsehoods, falsehoods into truths, and intermediates into intermediates. On these terms the law of excluded middle palpably fails. But we must remember, even while honoring this deviant logic as genuine logic, that the terminology 'true', 'false', and 'negation' carries over into it from our logic only by partial analogy. The failure of the law is, insofar, nominal.

By projecting the terminology along different analogies, might the law of excluded middle be nominally salvaged here still? It seems not. Call the new truth values 1, 2, 3. We can indeed group the values 2 and 3 under the joint heading 'false', and thus count each closed sentence still as "true" or "false." Or if, better, we continue to economize on terms by explaining falsity as truth of negation, the suggestion comes to this: value 1 is truth, and negation is to lead from the values 2 and 3 to 1 and from 1 to 2 or 3. But, if negation is to be a truth function at all, we must make up our mind: it must lead from 1 always to 2 or always to 3. Then, however, we forfeit the law of double negation. For, say negation leads from 1 always to 2; then double negation leads from 3 to 1 to 2 rather than back to 3. Thus we nominally salvage the law of excluded middle only by forfeiting double negation. Try what we will, three-valued logic turns out true to form: it is a rejection of the classical true-false dichotomy, or of classical negation.

It is hard to face up to the rejection of anything so basic. If anyone questions the meaningfulness of classical negation, we are tempted to say in defense that the negation of any given closed sentence is *explained* thus: it is true if and only if the given sentence is not true. This, we may feel, meets the charge of meaninglessness by providing meaning, and indeed a meaning that assures that any closed sentence or its negation is true. However, our defense here begs the question; let us give the dissident his due. In explaining the negation as true if and only if the given sentence is not true, we use the same classical 'not' that the dissident is rejecting.

Debate   Let us grant, then, that the deviant can coherently challenge
about the   our classical true-false dichotomy. But why should he want to?
dichotomy   Reasons over the years have ranged from bad to better. The worst one is that things are not just black and white; there are gradations. It is hard to believe that this would be seen as counting against classical negation; but irresponsible literature to this effect can be cited.

The next to worst one is a confusion between knowledge and truth. Certainly there is a vast intermediate domain of sentences between those that we know or even believe to be true and those that we know or believe to be false; but we can still hold that each of those intermediate sentences is either true, unbeknownst to us, or false unbeknownst to us. Perhaps part of the trouble is a confusion between (a) knowing something to be true or false and (b) knowing something to be true or knowing it to be false.

A more respectable reason for protesting the dichotomy has to do with the paradoxes of set theory and semantics. Thus take again Russell's paradoxical class $\{x: \sim(x \in x)\}$, and the sentence that says this class is a member of itself. The proposal is that we allow this and similar sentences the middle truth value. The equivalence, once so vexatious, of these sentences to their own negations, can thereupon be received with equanimity—negation now being, of course, the reformed negation of three-valued logic.

This proposal stems from Bočvar, 1939. In this case there is no underlying confusion, but still the plan is not to my liking. It runs counter to a generally sound strategy which I call the maxim of minimum mutilation. The classical logic of truth functions and quantification is free of paradox, and incidentally it is a paragon of clarity, elegance, and efficiency. The paradoxes emerge only with set theory and semantics. Let us then try to resolve them within set theory and semantics, and not lay fairer fields waste.

The next challenge to the law of excluded middle came out of physics: Heisenberg's paradoxical principle of indeterminacy in quantum mechanics. Certain magnitudes are incapable of being jointly ascertained, and this impossibility is a matter not merely of human frailty but of physical law. Under these circumstances it is wasteful and misleading to retain a logical apparatus that accommodates those empty questions. Birkhoff and von Neumann accordingly proposed, in 1936, a weakened substitute for truth-function logic. It lacks classical negation and, therewith, the law of excluded middle. It is not a many-valued logic; it is not truth-functional at all in structure. Alternative proposals by Rosser and by Destouches, to the same purpose, do use three-valued logic.

Most theoreticians of quantum mechanics have passed over these reforms. George Mackey has made some use of Birkhoff and von Neumann's logic. But Popper has lately argued that this logic cannot accomplish what it was meant for.

Whatever the technical merits of the case, I would cite again the maxim of minimum mutilation as a deterring consideration. I do place the claims of physics somewhat above those of set theory, because I see the justification of mathematics only in what it contributes to our integral science of nature. It is a question of remoteness from the data of observation; physics is less remote than set theory. But in any event let us not underestimate the price of a deviant logic. There is a serious loss of simplicity, especially when the new logic is not even a many-valued truth-functional logic. And there is a loss, still more serious, on the score of familiarity. Consider again the case, a page or so back, of begging the question in an attempt to defend classical negation. This only begins to illustrate the handicap of having to think within a deviant logic. The price is perhaps not quite prohibitive, but the returns had better be good.

We noticed a page back, as prompting a next to silliest objection to the law of excluded middle, a confusion between truth and knowledge. Now the present objection from quantum mechanics is in a way reminiscent of this, though without the confusion. It is an objection to any exorbitant excess of admissible questions over possible answers. Other things being equal, such an objection is sound; but we must weigh this excess against the gain in simplicity that it brings. Certainly the scientist admits as significant many sentences that are not linked in a distinctive way to any possible observations. He admits them so as to round out the theory and make it simpler, just as the arithmetician admits the irrational numbers so as to round out arithmetic and simplify computation; just, also, as the grammarian admits such sentences as Carnap's 'This stone is thinking about Vienna' and Russell's 'Quadruplicity drinks procrastination' so as to round out and simplify the grammar. Other things being equal, the less such fat the better; but when one begins to consider complicating logic to cut fat from quantum physics, I can believe that other things are far from equal. The fat must have been admirably serving its purpose of rounding out a smooth theory, and it is rather to be excused than excised.

The opposition to the law of excluded middle that is most widely known is not the one made on account of quantum mechanics. Rather it is that led by the mathematician L. E. J. Brouwer under the name of *intuitionism*. Here again the motive is diminution of the excess of accepted questions over possible answers. Intuitionists object, for instance, to affirming an alternation when the evidence is too indirect to suggest how to decide which one of the constituent sentences is true.

We had been picturing the rejection of the law of excluded middle, 'p or $\sim p$', mainly as rejection of classical negation. I have now directed the intuitionist's case rather at the alternation. Actually the distinction is unreal; once you upset the interrelations of the logical operators, you may be said to have revised any or all. Anyway, the intuitionist's negation is deviant also on its own account: the law of double negation lapses.

Let us remember that the names and notations of negation and alternation carry over to a deviant logic, such as that of intuitionism, only by a rough and somewhat arbitrary analogy. To revert to a distinction in Chapter 2, negation and alternation are immanent rather than transcendent. The intuitionist should not be viewed as controverting us as to the true laws of certain fixed logical operations, namely, negation and alternation. He should be viewed rather as opposing our negation and alternation as unscientific ideas, and propounding certain other ideas, somewhat analogous, of his own.

Intuitionist logic lacks the familiarity, the convenience, the simplicity, and the beauty of our logic. Like the logic of Birkhoff and von Neumann, intuitionist logic lacks the transparency even of a many-valued truth-functional logic. A kind of intuitive meaning is intended for its sentence connectives, and explained with help of words and phrases like 'refute' and 'follow from'; but these explanations go dim when one tries to respect the distinction between saying a sentence and talking about it. One does as well to bypass these explanations and go straight to Heyting's axiomatization of intuitionistic logic, thus learning the logic by what language teachers call direct method rather than by translation.

Intuitionism antedates Gödel's proof that there can be no complete proof procedure for number theory. This great result of Gödel's adds force, however, to the intuitionist protest. The excess of admitted questions over possible answers seems especially regrettable when the questions are mathematical and the answers mathematically impossible.

Intuitionism is one school of *constructivism*. More generally, constructivism in mathematics is intolerance of methods that lead to affirming the existence of things of some sort without showing how to find one. This is not a sharp definition of constructivism; there is none, or no unique one. My vague word 'find' could mean 'compute' in the case of a number, and 'construct', in some sense, in the case of a geometric figure or a set. Now constructivism, in some such sense, is congenial and admirable. Adherence to constructivist restraints makes for enhanced understanding of what we manage to accomplish within those restraints. Moreover, the paradoxes of set theory put an added premium on constructivism; for what we accomplish within its restraints is pretty clearly immune to the threat of contradiction that lingers outside. Even mathematicians who tolerate and use non-constructive methods recognize that a step forward has been made when a constructive proof is found for a theorem that had been proved non-constructively.

But one can practice and even preach a very considerable degree of constructivism without adopting intuitionist logic. Weyl's constructive set theory is nearly as old as Brouwer's intuitionism, and it uses orthodox logic; it goes constructivist only in its axioms of existence of sets. On this approach, constructivist scruples can be reconciled with the convenience and beauty of classical logic.

Up to now I have dwelt on deviations from the two-valued logic of truth functions. But deviance in logic extends to the quantifiers. As is to be expected from my recent vague characterization of constructivism, an existential quantification in the intuitionist's sense requires for its truth that a way be known of computing or somehow constructing a verifying instance. Insofar it differs from what we have called quantification.

An intimate connection between existential quantification and alternation, and between universal quantification and conjunction, is familiar and obvious. An existential quantification amounts to the alternation of its verifying singular sentences—or it would amount to that if the values available to the variable of quantification were finite in number and each had a name. Correspondingly for universal quantification and conjunction. Note that on this score the intuitionist's analogues of existential quantification and alternation pair off true to form. For, as lately mentioned, an intuitionist's alternation holds only if there is a way of finding one among its constituents that holds.

Any logic has to come to terms somehow with quantification, if it is not going to stop short. The literature contains developments not only of quantified intuitionist logic, but of quantified many-valued logic and quantified modal logic and, to some extent, the quantified logic of propositional attitudes. As hinted at the end of Chapter 2 and again at the end of Chapter 5, vexed questions arise over the significance of quantification in logics of the last two sorts.

The question of deviance in the logic of quantification is relevant to ontology—to the question what there is. What there are, according to a given theory in standard form, are all and only the objects that the variables of quantification are meant in that theory to take as values. This is scarcely contestable, since '(x)' and '$(\exists x)$' are explained by the words 'each object x is such that' and 'there is an object x such that'. Some languages may have no clear equivalent of our existential phrase 'there is', nor of our quantifiers; but surely there is no putting the two asunder.

Consequently some philosophical interest, ontological interest, attaches to deviations in quantification theory. They can affect what to count as there being. The intuitionist's deviant quantification (if 'quantification' is still a good word for it) carries with it a deviant notion of existence (if 'existence' is still a good word for it). When he says he recognizes there to be just such and such objects, we may not even agree that he recognizes there to be just those (much less that he would be right in so doing). It is only relative to some translation of his language into ours (not necessarily into our logic, but into our inclusive language) that *we* can venture to say what he really recognizes there to be (in *our* sense of 'there to be').

Branched quantifiers   In what remains of this chapter I shall be concerned with deviant quantification superimposed on the classical logic of truth functions. To perceive the motive for one of these departures, let us reflect briefly on clusters of quantifiers. The pair '$\forall x \, \exists y$' says that, for each choice of x, something y can be chosen fulfilling the appended condition. For different choices of x, different choices of y may be called for; in general the choice of y depends on that of x. But now consider the more complex case of some condition on x, y, z, and w, which we may picture as '$Fxyzw$'. Suppose we want to say that for each x there is a y, and for each z there is a w, such that $Fxyzw$. We want the choice of y to depend only on x, and the choice of w to depend only on z. But if we write:

$$(1) \qquad \forall x \, \exists y \, \forall z \, \exists w \, Fxyzw$$

we represent the choice of w as depending on x too; and if instead we write:

(2) $$\forall z \, \exists w \, \forall x \, \exists y \, Fxyzw$$

then we represent the choice of y as depending on z too. As a way of avoiding these unwanted dependences, the branching notation:

(3) $$\begin{matrix} \forall x \, \exists y \\ \forall z \, \exists w \end{matrix} \, Fxyzw$$

suggests itself. It can be shown that (1) and (2) are not logically equivalent; and now (3) is a third thing, equivalent to neither. Acceptance of (3) and other branching quantifications is a logical deviation of a supplementing kind, like the annexes noted late in Chapter 5. But this supplementation is unlike those in being so strikingly continuous with what it supplements.

If we quantify over functions, we can get (3) back into line thus:

(4) $$\exists f \, \exists g \, \forall x \, \forall z \, Fx(fx)z(gz).$$

But here we affirm the existence of abstract objects of a certain sort: functions. We leave logic and ascend into a mathematics of functions, which can be reduced to set theory but not to pure logic.

This example clearly reflects the ontological relevance of any strengthening of the logic of quantification. The effect of (3) is that the services of certain abstract objects, namely functions, are gained without recognizing these functions as objects. The ramified formula (3) does the work of the mathematical formula (4), though the variables in (3) do not require functions as values.

One might think it a shortcoming of classical quantification that required us to ascend to the mathematical formula (4). One might think it unfair to impute the assumption of abstract objects to someone who makes this ascent just to make his variable 'y' independent of 'z'. One who thinks this will adopt the ramified notation (3) so as not to acknowledge these abstract objects.

But on the other hand there is reason, and better reason, to feel that our previous conception of quantification which excludes (3) is not capriciously narrow. On the contrary, it determines an integrated domain of logical theory with bold and significant boundaries, designate it as we may. One manifestation of the boldness of these boundaries is the following. The logic of quantification in its unsupplemented form admits of complete proof procedures for validity ((B) of Chapter 4). It also admits of complete proof procedures for inconsistency; for, to prove a schema inconsistent we have only to prove its negation valid. Now a remarkable fact which emerges from findings of Craig, Henkin, and others is that as soon as you branch out in the manner of (3) you get into a terrain that does not admit simultaneously of complete proof procedures for validity and inconsistency.[1]

This is not to say of course that every liberalization of the classical notation of quantification would obstruct completeness. A liberalization that added only finitely many valid or inconsistent formulas, for instance, could have no such effect. The special significance of the example (3) lay rather in the suspicion that in excluding (3) our classical logic of quantification was capriciously restrictive. Considerations of completeness of proof procedures have served to counter this suspicion by showing that (3) is a more abrupt departure than it seemed.

A remarkable concurrence of diverse definitions of logical truth, in Chapter 4, already suggested to us that the logic of quantification as classically bounded is a solid and significant unity. Our present reflections on branching quantification further confirm this impression. It is at the limits of the classical logic of quantification, then, that I would continue to draw the line between logic and mathematics. Such, also, is the concept of quantification by which I would assess a theory's ontological demands. In particular, thus, instead of viewing (3) as coordinate with (1) and (2), I would view (3) as a mathematical formula whose ontological content is fairly shown in (4).

Substitutional quantification   We reflected lately on the connection between existential quantification and alternation. If all the objects are named and finite in number, the quantification is of course dispensable in favor of alternation, and can be viewed as a mere abbreviation. If the objects are infinite in number, on the other hand, this expansion would require an infinitely long alternation. Midway in Chapter 4 we arrived at a view of expressions as finite sequences, in a mathematical sense; and the further step to infinite sequences is in no way audacious. It would, however, be distinctly a departure from all writings on grammar and most writings on logic, including this book, to invoke infinite expressions. Existential quantification over an infinite universe is not dispensable in favor of our alternation notation: finite alternation.

But existential quantification over an infinite universe still ad-

[1] See "Existence and quantification," in my *Ontological Relativity and Other Essays* (New York: Columbia Univ., 1969).

mits of an attractive semantical explanation or truth condition, even though not of elimination, so long as all the objects have names. The quantification is true if and only if at least one of its instances—got by dropping the quantifier and putting a name for the variable—is true.

All this about existential quantification holds equally, *mutatis mutandis*, for universal quantification. As long as all objects have names, a universal quantification is true if and only if all its instances are true.

Our standard logical grammar, at its strictest, admitted no names (Chapter 2). Names can be simulated by contextual definition; this was why we could do without names in our strictest standard grammar. This way of providing for names does not go very well with these semantical explanations of quantification, however, since quantification is needed already in the contextual definition. So we will do well for the space of the present discussion to think in terms rather of standard logical grammar in the broader sense, admitting names.

These truth conditions for quantification, based on substitution of names for variables, have been favored by Ruth Marcus and others. They compare and contrast curiously with the Tarskian one seen in (5) of Chapter 3. They do share the sort of circularity that was already remarked on midway in Chapter 3: the existential quantification is true if *some* instance is true, and the universal quantification is true if *every* instance is true. But the great contrast is that (5) of Chapter 3 speaks only of values of variables and makes no appeal to names. For this, (5) pays a price in complexity.

Thus far, no deviation; just different characterizations of the same quantification, so long as everything has a name. But now it must be remarked that this last is a very restrictive condition, even given our provisional new readiness to admit names. In a generous universe there are more things than can be named even with an infinitude of names. For, let us recall again one of the twin discrepancies noted in Chapter 4 between sets and open sentences. We saw that some of the sets are not determined by any of the sentences. But these sets will lack names; for if a set has a name, say 'a', then the set is determined by the sentence '$x \in a$'.

A more customary argument to the same purpose makes reference to a classical theorem of set theory, which says that the irrational numbers cannot all be assigned distinct integers. In contrast, all names can be assigned distinct integers, for instance in Gödel's way. It follows that the irrational numbers cannot all be assigned distinct names.

We saw in Chapter 4 that the substitutional definition of logical truth came out coextensive with the model-theoretic definition of logical truth, so long as the object language was rich enough in vocabulary. We now see that an opposite sort of situation holds for quantification: the substitutional characterization of quantification is not coextensive with the characterization in terms of objects, or values of variables, if we assume a rich universe. An existential quantification could turn out false when substitutionally construed and true when objectually construed, because of there being objects of the purported kind but only nameless ones. A universal quantification could turn out false when objectually construed and true when substitutionally construed, because of there being objects to the contrary but only nameless ones. And no lavishness with names can prevent there being nameless objects in a generous universe. Substitutional quantification is deviant if the universe is rich.

Its strength   The deviation just now noted consists in leaving certain objects out of account, namely, those without names. But substitutional quantification can deviate also in an opposite way: the substituted expressions can fail to name. The truth condition that we formulated for substitutional quantification spoke expressly of the substitution of names, but it would work for any other grammatical category as well as for the category of names. If the category is finite, then the quantifications are again of course eliminable in favor of alternations and conjunctions. We saw a case of precisely this already in the latter part of Chapter 5, in the eliminable quantification of the variables 'α', 'β', etc., in the positions of a hundred one-place predicates. It is interesting to note now an extension of that eliminable brand of quantification, in the form of an uneliminable brand of substitutional quantification. It builds upon the virtual theory of classes (Chapter 5), and the names that it draws upon in substitution for its variables 'α', 'β', etc. are the contextually defined abstracts of the virtual theory. If the resulting quantification over stimulated classes is seen as cause for rejoicing, then let me remind you in sorrow that these quantifiers are no mere manner of speaking. They are nicely explained, but they are not eliminably defined. Moreover, because virtual class abstracts and the corresponding variables come only after 'ϵ', the domain of classes afforded is insufficient foundation for any appreciable mathematics.

When some new brand of quantification is introduced by definition, and thus eliminable, it of course does not commit us really to recognizing any objects as values of the variables. It is simulated quantification with a simulated ontological commitment. Our real commitment rests rather with the real quantifiers in the standard language that backs up those false fronts of contextual definition. And note the importance of this stipulation that the grammar be standard. If modalities or other constructions are admitted in addition to truth functions and quantifiers, they add to the strength or content of the theories in ways that are incommensurable with what might be got by enlarging the universe; incommensurable, that is, except relative to some translation of the whole into standard grammar.

Substitutional quantification, on the other hand, is neither an eliminable simulation nor a genuine objectual quantification (unless, of course, all things have names). It is not a way, then, of getting along with a null ontology, an empty universe; it is a non-standard idiom, rather, foreign to the language in which we talk of what there is and of values of variables. If one does still happen to wonder what would be an adequate universe for some theory that comes to him in this non-standard idiom, the thing for him to do is seek one or another reasonable-looking paraphrase of the theory into a standard form in which quantification is objectually construed. Then he can assess the universe of this theory—though the various passable translations may well call for different universes. An unimaginative way of thus translating substitutional quantification is to translate it into a metalanguage in which we talk of strings of signs and concatenation and substitution and truth—the sort of language touched on midway in Chapter 3. Identifying the strings with numbers as Gödel did, we end up with the positive integers as universe.

THE GROUND OF

LOGICAL TRUTH

My most general definition of logical truth, at the end of
Chapter 4, rested on two things: grammar, which is a purely
linguistic affair, and truth, which is not. A sentence is logically
true if all sentences with that grammatical structure are true.

In other words, one is tempted to say, a sentence is logically
true if true by virtue purely of its grammatical structure. I avoid
this phrasing, for it suggests that it is language that makes logical
truths true—purely language, and nothing to do with the nature of
the world. This doctrine, which I call the linguistic theory of logical
truth, is one that Carnap subscribed to. But I think there is less to it
than meets the eye.

Granted, grammatical structure is linguistic; but so is lexicon.
The lexicon is used in talking about the world; but so is grammatical
structure. A logical truth, staying true as it does under all lexical
substitutions, admittedly depends upon none of those features of the
world that are reflected in lexical distinctions; but may it not depend
on other features of the world, features that our language reflects in
its grammatical constructions rather than its lexicon? It would be
pointless to protest that grammar varies from language to language,
for so does lexicon. Perhaps the logical truths owe their truth to
certain traits of reality which are reflected in one way by the grammar of our language, in another way by the grammar of another
language, and in a third way by the combined grammar and lexicon
of a third language.

We may recall from Chapter 2 that the very distinction between grammar and lexicon is immanent, and admits of alternative

adjustments even in the analysis of one and the same language. As this distinction varies, the distinction between logical truth and other truth varies with it. Insofar, the demarcation of logical truth rests on the whim of the descriptive grammarian. Now one would hesitate to let a sentence vacillate between being true purely by virtue of the language and being true partly by virtue of the nature of the world, according as the grammarian chooses to describe our already existing language in one or other of two permissible ways. Or perhaps one could handle this by counting all the sentences as true purely by virtue of language (in a word: as *analytic*) that come out logically true under any of the various admissible grammatical descriptions of the language. However, it is time to rein in our verbalism. What are we trying to get at when we call a sentence analytic, or true purely by virtue of the language?

When we ask this question, our focus changes. Our focus shifts to the phrase 'true by virtue of'. How, given certain circumstances and a certain true sentence, might we hope to show that the sentence was true by virtue of those circumstances? If we could show that the sentence was logically implied by sentences describing those circumstances, could more be asked? But any sentence logically implies the logical truths. Trivially, then, the logical truths are true by virtue of any circumstances you care to name—language, the world, anything.

Is logic a compendium of the broadest traits of reality, or is it just an effect of linguistic convention? Must all right-minded men agree on logic, or is it every language for itself? These are resonant questions. They seem to resound to the deepest level of the philosophy of logic. Clearly the two questions are in close harmony; almost they are two forms of a single question. Just now the first of the two questions, or forms, has proved unsound; or all sound, signifying nothing. As for the second question, or form, it proved empty early in Chapter 6. The logics of two cultures will be, we saw, incommensurable at worst and never in conflict, since conflict would simply discredit our translation. The same attitude would apply, we noted, even to a logical deviant within our linguistic community: we would account his deviation a difference of dialect.

That logic is thus tied to translation does, on the face of it, conspicuously favor the linguistic theory of logical truth. Yet we find that theory empty of content. This pair of circumstances ceases to be puzzling when we recall why logic is inseparable from translation. The reason is just that logic is obvious; potentially obvious. Logical truths are tied to translation in no deeper sense, I argued, than other obvious truths, e.g., utterances of 'It is raining' in the rain.

In calling logical truths obvious, or potentially obvious, I am not explaining why they are true or how we learn them. My point is just that there is no *added* significance in the inseparability of logic and translation. Obviousness, whatever its cause, would already make for that inseparability. One is tempted to infer a linguistic theory of logical truth from that inseparability, and not to infer it from the mere fact of obviousness; this is the mistake.

The two collapses that we have been viewing in these last pages are much alike in form and effect. (1) Logic is true by virtue of language only as, vacuously, it is true by virtue of anything and everything. (2) Logic is inseparable from translation only as anything obvious is inseparable from translation.

A further circumstance that makes people think of logic as peculiarly a matter of language was noted already at the end of Chapter 1 and the beginning of Chapter 2: the circumstance of oblique generalization. It prompts us to talk about sentences, and hence language. There are those who, intent rather on separating logic from language, have interposed propositions in a nonlinguistic sense of the word. Their motive of separating logic from language is more to be applauded than their shabby expedient. And even their motive is not much to be applauded, for, as urged in those pages, the truth predicate is already present and doing an active job of separating logic from language. The truth predicate serves the crucial purpose, in oblique generalization, of disquotation. Logical theory, despite its heavy dependence on talk of language, is already world-oriented rather than language-oriented; and the truth predicate makes it so.

We have noticed close bonds between logic and language. There is this matter of oblique generalization by semantic ascent. There is the role of grammatical structure in distinguishing logical truths from other truths. There is the respect for logic in translation. We have noticed also the tendency to imagine between logic and language a still closer bond than we can make proper sense of; namely, the linguistic doctrine of logical truth, the idea that logic is analytic.

An untenable dualism   At a more general level, we may note also three circumstances which encourage the expectation at least that logic is grounded differently from the natural sciences, even if one put aside any specifically linguistic theory of logical truth. One of these circumstances is the remarkable obviousness or potential obviousness of logical truth. We saw how this circumstance could wrongly encourage a linguistic theory of logical truth; but, even when that mistake is not made, the circumstance is one that sets logic conspicuously apart from other sciences. A second circumstance is the lack of special subject matter: logic favors no distinctive portion of the lexicon, and neither does it favor one subdomain of values of variables over another. A third circumstance is the ubiquity of the use of logic. It is a handmaiden of all the sciences, including mathematics.

It is interesting to compare mathematics with logic on these three counts. Mathematics, surely, even elementary number theory, is not potentially obvious throughout; it does not even admit of a complete proof procedure. Considerable parts of mathematics are potentially obvious. Other large parts are accessible from unobvious beginnings by individually obvious steps; but we must bear in mind that those are steps mostly of logic. Insofar, what stands forth is less a kinship of mathematics to logic than the extreme efficacy of logic as handmaiden to mathematics.

On the second count, again, mathematics is intermediate. Mathematics has its favored lexicon, unlike logic, and its distinctively relevant values of variables. But, despite all this, mathematics presents as impartial a front to natural science as logic does. For the distinctive terms and the distinctive objects of mathematics tend mostly to favor one branch of natural science no more than another.

On the third count, finally, versatile ancillarity, mathematics is admirable. It is a handmaiden to some extent of all natural sciences, and to a serious extent of many. We might say at the risk of marring the figure that it is their promiscuity, in this regard, that goes far to distinguish logic and mathematics from other sciences.

Because of these last two traits of logic and mathematics—their relevance to all science and their partiality toward none—it is customary to draw an emphatic boundary separating them from the natural sciences. These latter are seen as monopolizing the information; logic and mathematics serve only in processing it. This account is an arresting one, but the trouble comes in pressing it beyond the stage of metaphor. What clear notion of information would fit the account? Early in Chapter 1 we speculated on two august notions of information, one of them cosmological and the other epistemological. One was the distribution of microphysical states and the other was the distribution of sensory elements. If each sentence of science could be assigned its individual share of information in either of these senses, the doctrine of analyticity would be sustained: the analytic sentences would include the truths of logic and mathematics, and would be distinguished from truths of nature by their lack of information. Where the myth lies, however, is in the notion of any such general sorting of information over sentences.

Once a boundary is drawn thus emphatically between the natural sciences on the one hand and logic and mathematics on the other, an effect is that all the evidence of the senses comes to be credited to the natural sciences. Logic and mathematics are regarded as untouched by it. They are permitted to serve the natural sciences, but there is no thought, conversely, of any corroboration of logic or mathematics by the success of these services. The curtain that separates the natural sciences, on the one hand, from logic and mathematics on the other, is a one-way screen.

Not that the truths of logic or mathematics come to be doubted in consequence of this lack of acknowledged empirical support. On the contrary, one is too generous. One views these domains as immune likewise to empirical refutation. What I am deploring is not a lack of justice toward logic and mathematics. It is the division.

One tends to forget how remote some theories can lie from any indirectly relevant observational evidence, and still be classed as physics. A bit of physical theory can be shot through with mathematics, but it will still be classed as physics as long as it keeps a mixed lexicon. What any such bit of physics contributes to the coherence of the rest of physical theory, and so to the organization, indirectly and ultimately, of the data of observation, will redound to its own credit as indirect empirical evidence of its truth. But the mathematical and logical component, purified of all physical lexicon, is not called physics. Whatever remote links this component had with observation, through functioning as part of a context of theoretical physics, are seen as empirical evidence only for the recognized physical part of the context.

The mistake comes of responding excessively to the terminological boundaries between sciences. Instead of viewing empirical evidence as evidence for the whole interlocked scientific system, including mathematics and logic as integral parts, people think of the evidence as seeping through the system only as far as the interface between what they call theoretical physics and what they call mathematics.

No wonder, then, that they cast about for some different ground of mathematical truth, and of logical truth. Here are the firmest of the sciences, and not a shred of empirical evidence is allowed them. Other causes which we have reviewed and deplored in recent pages will already have encouraged those philosophers in a linguistic theory of logical truth. Finding mathematics and logic behind the barrier together, they adopt the linguistic theory for both.

The place   Some there are, indeed, who have urged on the contrary that
of logic   arithmetic is directly supported by observation. You put seven
rabbits in a pen, add five more, and for a while the total is twelve. When I speak for a kinship between mathematics and natural science I do not mean this. The ' + ' of '7 + 5' should connote no spatial assembling of objects, let alone any stability of rabbit-count through time. If at a certain moment there are seven rabbits in a certain region and five rabbits in a certain region, and the two regions do not overlap, then at that moment there are twelve rabbits in the region, quite possibly discontinuous, which consists of those two regions. This is the most that can be said of rabbits on the strength of '7 + 5 = 12'.

The kinship I speak for is rather a kinship with the most general and systematic aspects of natural science, farthest from observation. Mathematics and logic are supported by observation only in the indirect way that those aspects of natural science are supported by observation; namely, as participating in an organized whole which, way up at its empirical edges, squares with observation. I am concerned to urge the empirical character of logic and mathematics no more than the unempirical character of theoretical physics; it is rather their kinship that I am urging, and a doctrine of gradualism.

A case in point was seen midway in Chapter 6, in the proposal to change logic to help quantum mechanics. The merits of the proposal may be dubious, but what is relevant just now is that such proposals have been made. Logic is in principle no less open to revision than quantum mechanics or the theory of relativity. The goal is, in each, a world system—in Newton's phrase—that is as smooth and simple as may be and that nicely accommodates observations around the edges. If revisions are seldom proposed that cut so deep as to touch logic, there is a clear enough reason for that: the maxim of minimum mutilation (Chapter 6). The maxim suffices to explain the air of necessity that attaches to logical and mathematical truth.

This much can be said for the linguistic theory of logical truth: we learn logic in learning language. But this circumstance does not distinguish logic from vast tracts of common-sense knowledge that would generally be called empirical. There is no clear way of separating our knowledge into one part that consists merely in knowing the language and another part that goes beyond. Obviously the truth of the most casually factual sentence depends partly on language;

the use of the syllable 'killed' in our language could have been such as to make 'Brutus killed Caesar' come out false. But the boundary between the sentences that are true purely by virtue of language, or analytic, and those that are true only partly by virtue of language, is the boundary that has seemed at length to waver and dissolve.

Carnap, in his linguistic theory of logical truth, has represented language as analogous to a formal deductive system: there are *formation* rules and *transformation* rules. The formation rules give the grammar and lexicon. They are the analogues of the rules of a formal deductive system that specify the notation of the system—the rules that specify what Church calls the well-formed formulas. The transformation rules give the logical truths (also the mathematical truths, indeed the analytic truths generally). They are the analogues of the axioms and rules of inference of a formal deductive system. Grammar and logic are thus, for Carnap, on an equal footing; a language has its grammar and its logic.

Carnap sees the analogy of languages to formal deductive systems only as an analogy, and recognizes that neither the transformation rules nor the formation rules are explicit in the minds of those who learn a language as native speakers. But my position, despite my emphasis on the intimate connection between grammar and logic, is that this analogy is unhelpful at best.

We do better to abandon this analogy and think in terms rather of how a child actually acquires his language and all those truths or beliefs, of whatever kind, that he acquires along with it. The truths or beliefs thus acquired are not limited to logical truths, nor to mathematical truths, nor even to analytic truths, if we suppose some sense made of this last term. Among these truths and beliefs the logical truths are to be distinguished only by the fact, it will be recalled, that all other sentences with the same grammatical structure are true too.

Seen from this point of view the various salient traits of the logical truths go naturally together. For consider, to begin with, the place of grammar in language. Anyone who is said to have learned a language (that language and not some related dialect) will have learned its grammar. Those who know the language vary in vocabulary, that is, in what they know of the lexicon, according to their interests and education; but they have the grammar in common. Whoever deviates from the grammar is to be classed either as a foreigner who has not mastered the language or as a native whose dialect is different. All who use the language use the same grammatical constructions, whatever be the subject and whatever the applicable quarter of the lexicon. So the logical truths, being tied to the grammar and not to the lexicon, will be among the truths on which all speakers are likeliest to agree (if we disregard examples that engender confusion through sheer complexity). For it is only lexicon, not grammar, that registers differences in background from speaker to speaker; and the logical truths stay true under all lexical substitutions. Naturally the habit of accepting these truths will be acquired hand in hand with grammatical habits. Naturally therefore the logical truths, or the simple ones, will go without saying; everyone will unhesitatingly assent to them if asked. Logical truths will qualify as obvious, in the behavioral sense in which I am using this term, or potentially obvious.

A second salient trait of the logical truths was seen in our tendency, in generalizing over them, to resort to semantic ascent. This again is explained by the invariance of logical truth under lexical substitutions. The only sort of generality that can be managed by quantifying within the object language, and thus without semantic ascent, is generality that keeps the predicates fixed and generalizes only over the values of the subject variables. If we are to vary the predicates too, as for logical theory we must, the avenue is semantic ascent.

A third salient trait was the universal applicability of logic, its impartial participation in all the sciences. This again is explained by the invariance of logical truth under lexical substitutions. The lexicon is what caters distinctively to special tastes and interests. Grammar and logic are the central facility, serving all comers.

Chapter 1 *Meaning and Truth*

Quine, W. V., *Ontological Relativity and Other Essays*, essays 1, 3, and 6. New York: Columbia University Press, 1969.
——, *Word and Object*, chaps. I and II. Cambridge, Mass.: M.I.T. Press, 1960.

Chapter 2 *Grammar*

Chomsky, Noam, *Syntactic Structures*. The Hague: Mouton, 1957.
Davidson, Donald, "The logical form of action sentences," in *The Logic of Action and Preference*, ed. Nicholas Rescher. Pittsburgh: University Press, 1967.
Føllesdal, Dagfinn, "Knowledge, identity, and existence," *Theoria*, 33 (1967), 1-27.
Hiż, Henry, "The intuitions of grammatical categories," *Methodos*, 12 (1960), 311-19.
Quine, W. V., *Elementary Logic*, rev. ed. Cambridge, Mass.: Harvard University Press, 1966.
——, *From a Logical Point of View*, 2nd ed., essays III and VIII. Cambridge, Mass.: Harvard University Press, 1961.
——, *Methods of Logic*, 4th ed. Cambridge, Mass.: Harvard University Press, 1982.
——, *Selected Logic Papers*, paper XXIII. New York: Random House, 1966.
——, *Word and Object*, chaps. V and VI.

Chapter 3 *Truth*

Quine, W. V., *Mathematical Logic*, rev. ed., sec. 6 and chap. VII. Cambridge, Mass.: Harvard University Press, 1951.

————, *Set Theory and Its Logic*, rev. ed., chaps. I-IV. Cambridge, Mass.: Harvard University Press, 1969.

Tarski, Alfred, "The concept of truth in formalized languages," in *Logic, Semantics, Metamathematics*, pp. 152-278. Oxford: Clarendon Press, 1956. This is a translation of the German version of 1936.

Chapter 4 *Logical Truth*

Quine, W. V., *Selected Logic Papers*, papers II and XIX.

Van Heijenoort, Jean, ed., *From Frege to Gödel*, pp. 508-24, 578-616. Cambridge, Mass.: Harvard University Press, 1967.

Chapter 5 *The Scope of Logic*

Feys, Robert, *Modal Logic*. Paris: Gauthier-Villars, 1965.

Martin, Richard M., "A homogeneous system for formal logic," *Journal of Symbolic Logic*, 8 (1943), 1-23.

Quine, W. V., *Set Theory and Its Logic*, chap. XI.

Chapter 6 *Deviant Logics*

Birkhoff, Garrett, and John von Neumann, "The logic of quantum mechanics," *Annals of Mathematics*, 37 (1936), 823-43.

Heyting, Arend, *Intuitionism*. Amsterdam: North-Holland, 1956.

Marcus, Ruth B., "Modalities and intensional languages," *Synthese*, 13 (1961), 303-22.

Popper, Karl R., "Birkhoff and von Neumann's interpretation of quantum mechanics," *Nature*, 219 (1968), 682-85.

Quine, W. V., *Ontological Relativity*, essay 4.

Rosser, J. Barkley, and Atwell R. Turquette, *Many-Valued Logics*. Amsterdam: North-Holland, 1952.

Van Heijenoort, Jean, ed., *From Frege to Gödel*, pp. 446-63.

Weyl, Hermann, *Das Kontinuum* (1918). New York: Chelsea, 1960.

Chapter 7 *The Ground of Logical Truth*

Carnap, Rudolf, *Philosophy and Logical Syntax*. London: Routledge & Kegan Paul, 1935.

Quine, W. V., *From a Logical Point of View*, essay II.

————, *The Ways of Paradox and Other Essays*, enlarged ed., essay 12. Cambridge, Mass.: Harvard University Press, 1976.

White, Morton, "The analytic and the synthetic: an untenable dualism," in *John Dewey: Philosopher of Science and Freedom*, ed. S. Hook. New York: Dial, 1950.

A

B

C